Life and Work Express

David Firth

■ Fast track route to getting your life-work balance right

■ Covers all the key aspects of the work-home-self triangle, from knowing when and how to say 'no' and trusting your intuition to setting compelling goals and loose boundaries

■ Packed with lessons and tips from well balanced companies, including SAS, Ernst & Young and Capital One, and ideas from life-work gurus such as Daryl Conner, Charles Handy, Richard Pascale and Ed Schein

■ Includes a glossary of key concepts and a comprehensive resources guide

LIFE & WORK

10.01

≫EXPRESS EXEC. COM≪
essential management thinking at your fingertips

The right of David Firth to be identified as the author of this work has been
asserted in accordance with the Copyright, Designs and Patents Act 1988

First published 2002 by
Capstone Publishing (a Wiley company)
8 Newtec Place
Magdalen Road
Oxford OX4 1RE
United Kingdom
http://www.capstoneideas.com

CIP catalogue records for this book are available from the British Library and the
US Library of Congress

ISBN 1-84112-389-7

This book is printed on acid-free paper

Substantial discounts on bulk quantities of Capstone books are available
to corporations, professional associations and other organizations. Please
contact Capstone for more details on +44 (0)1865 798 623 or (fax) +44
(0)1865 240 941 or (e-mail) info@wiley-capstone.co.uk

Contents

For my father.

"... devising it all for Company..."

Samuel Beckett

"Who first invented work, and bound the free
And holiday-rejoicing spirit down
To that dry drudgery at the desk's dead wood?"

Charles Lamb

"O thou good Kent! how shall I live and work
To match thy goodness? My life will be too short,
And every measure fail me."

Cordelia Act IV Sc vii *King Lear*

Introduction to ExpressExec

ExpressExec is 3 million words of the latest management thinking compiled into 10 modules. Each module contains 10 individual titles forming a comprehensive resource of current business practice written by leading practitioners in their field. From brand management to balanced scorecard, ExpressExec enables you to grasp the key concepts behind each subject and implement the theory immediately. Each of the 100 titles is available in print and electronic formats.

Through the ExpressExec.com Website you will discover that you can access the complete resource in a number of ways:

» printed books or e-books;
» e-content – PDF or XML (for licensed syndication) adding value to an intranet or Internet site;
» a corporate e-learning/knowledge management solution providing a cost-effective platform for developing skills and sharing knowledge within an organization;
» bespoke delivery – tailored solutions to solve your need.

Why not visit www.expressexec.com and register for free key management briefings, a monthly newsletter and interactive skills checklists. Share your ideas about ExpressExec and your thoughts about business today.

Please contact elound@wiley-capstone.co.uk for more information.

Introduction to Life and Work

How do people think about their lives at work in today's world? What are the pressures that force individuals to reinvent their relationship to work? What is influencing organizations to redesign their management practices and thus place their people at the heart of business? This chapter sets the scene:

» if there was ever a job for life, it's gone now
» a world created by work is changing – so work has changed too
» self-responsibility is the key

My father worked for the same company for 30-odd years. He would leave the house ten minutes before he was due to start work (you'll understand that there was less traffic in those days) and be home again at the end of the day by five-thirty. In between, he would come home for his lunch for one hour, including travel time. I too would come home from school for lunch, though interestingly this is not a title about life and education or school/life balance. We ate lunch together as a family. Every day.

Only once, when my father, in the twilight of his career, was taken off the board of directors at his company and replaced by an up-and-coming bright young thing, did work present itself in our lives as anything other than:

» the means to bring money into the household, and
» a place that my father went in the mornings and left behind in the evenings.

What it presented itself as that one time was these things:

» a source of pride and dignity,
» a measure of personal achievement, and
» an expression of one's identity and relationship to the world.

And what work provoked my father to confront that Tuesday evening almost a quarter of a century ago were some big questions about life which hitherto I had not dreamt were in any way related to the world of work; namely "is change a bad thing or can it be the source of good too?"; "do I have the energy to fight and the depth to learn from this change?"; "what am I worth?"; "how is my worth signaled in the world?" and "what does it mean to grow old?"

I think these and many other life questions are faced by most of us at some point during our working lives – still others are faced after we "retire" altogether from work. I guess in truth that these sorts of questions were being faced by my father and his peers pretty much regularly throughout their working lives – it's simply that a combination of social mores and individual personality meant that my father did a good job of keeping them out of our domestic setting. Things are different now.

They tell us that there was just as much sexual abuse of children a generation ago as there is now – it's just that we're better at talking about it now, better at letting on to each other that we all know about the big secret. I think that the same is true about life and work. Now we seem to be fascinated to know what work means, what role it plays in our lives and how these two things feed each other. More and more, people realize that work is not a place to go, but something that they do over which they have a great degree of control, not only in terms of when and where they work but also how they engage with process and task. The kinds of work being done now are dramatically different from that in my father's generation. The experience of work is different (few regular days and one-hour lunch breaks now). So too are attitudes towards and expectations of work vastly changed.

And that's why this title exists in the ExecExpress series.

But life and work is an enormous, unwieldy subject. What focus will we take in this title? That is the subject of the next chapter.

What is Life and Work?

This chapter examines the three intertwined strands, which constitute life and work:

» it's an enquiry into the relationship of work and life – what work is for and the role it plays in your life
» it's about the balance between life and work – and how organizations and individuals can get it right
» it's about taking responsibility for your working life by optimizing the way you manage yourself – from stress and health issues through travel and telecommuting to career management and lifelong learning.

"Something is happening and it affects us all . . ."
Fast Company issue 1 November, 1995

In 1963, the Beatles and Lady Chatterley virtually invented sex, joked the poet Philip Larkin. And 32 years later, business reinvented itself as the new rock and roll.

In the last months of 1995, an American business magazine naming itself *Fast Company* unleashed itself upon the world with a new agenda. The founding editors, deliberately invoking in that description of themselves a nation's memory of frontier days and manifest destiny, set out their analysis of a brave new world:

> "A global revolution is changing business, and business is changing the world. With unsettling speed, two forces are converging: a new generation of business leaders is rewriting the rules of business, and a new breed of fast companies is challenging the corporate status quo.
>
> "That convergence overturns 50 years of received wisdom on the fundamentals of work and competition. No part of business is immune. The structure of the company is changing; relationships between companies are changing; the nature of work is changing; the definition of success is changing. The result is a revolution as far-reaching as the Industrial Revolution."

And these founding fathers gave themselves a role to play, a call to action:

> "Here's What We've Set Out To Do:
>
> » Accurately, honestly, and entertainingly identify the knowledge workers, management innovators, and idea merchants leading the business revolution. Our new community is waiting to emerge and converge. We mean to have serious fun. All we need is the meeting ground.
> » Create the language of the revolution: a new business vocabulary that captures and expresses our common experiences, the common language we use to talk to each other.

» Identify the values of the revolution and the people who are building companies that embody them: a commitment to merge economic growth with social justice, democratic participation with tough-minded execution, explosive technological innovation with old-fashioned individual commitment.

» Debunk old myths and discover new legends – before they're celebrified beyond recognition. A new community needs its own legitimate heroes and heroines, its models and mentors. At the same time, it's open season on pretenders, phonies, and purveyors of business snake oil.

» Start conversations, stimulate debates, provoke arguments, create healthy tension. Fast Company will be the first – not the last – word in cutting-edge business thinking. If you find something to apply in your work, something to talk about with your colleagues, something to help reframe a problem, something to disagree with, then Fast Company is succeeding.''

[A few years later the leading geek magazine of the new technological revolution, *Wired*, gave itself a manifesto too. It was hip to be an insurgent, but better for the credibility if you had a credo.]

Fast Company clearly hit a chord with both the baby boomers and the Generation Xers: the magazine became a cool brand (you can buy the *FC* travel umbrella – ''be both hip and dry!'' – at https://store.fast-company.com/cgi-bin/store/1138.html). Sales – and with it advertising revenues – sky-rocketed and readers – ''members of the *FC* Community'' – formed themselves into self-help/support/networking/best-practice-sharing clubs called The Company of Friends (there are currently over 150 ''cells'' across the world with a total membership of 39,000). It offered itself as the reading material to be seen with to a world of work which had hitherto had access only to magazines such as the brilliant but stuffy *Harvard Business Review*. *Fast Company* happened to launch itself right at the start of the Internet age, but they were always going to be about the ''new'' in the ''new economy''.

Above all, *Fast Company* made it okay to talk about what work meant, to talk about how work can satisfy personal development needs, how it can be a huge canvass for one's creativity and talents. In the late nineties, there was a buzz about life and work and new ways of organizing businesses around the human being, which *Fast*

Company tapped into with accuracy and sensitivity. That it coincided with and was fuelled by the Internet boom was a significant part of the excitement. Everything seemed possible. We could at last create smart organizations that truly valued the talents of the people they employed – and we could become very rich overnight into the bargain.

But times change.

By August 2001, struggling to find new ways to be passionate and evangelical in the midst of a sobering US economic slowdown, *Fast Company* still reassures us that the "new economy" is alive and well, in one area at least:

> "After decades of thinking that 'business' was synonymous with 'the corporation' and that workers were anonymous cogs in a giant machine, we have come to understand that the new unit of analysis for creating value, making change, and producing results is the unit of one.
>
> "One person with one great idea is the fuel that powers the new economy. That person may be an evangelist for change inside a vast, global corporation, the leader of a high-energy start-up, or the sole creator of a Website that attracts millions of visitors. Never before in the history of business has each person mattered more – as a talented performer, as a leader in an organization, as a consumer in the market, as a creator in the world of enterprise."

FAST COMPANY ONLINE: THE STATE OF THE NEW ECONOMY

This emancipation of the individual, though, seemed always to be just that – a revolution for the individual rather than for some greater good of society. This was no new communism. This was about personal pleasure and achievement in all its forms. And make no mistake, work in the late nineties brought a whole wealth of more material satisfactions.

As *Fast Company* flourished and was joined by the likes of *Business 2.0* and *Red Herring*, glamorizing the new world of work, so too did work itself become a topic fit for discussing in what were hitherto seen as purely leisure publications. The media was reflecting the reality that the boundaries between work and life (or lifestyle) were becoming significantly blurred.

In the UK, *FHM*, *GQ* and *Later* all celebrated the "new work", asking (and giving answers to) questions such as: "what salary should you be on?" and "what's cool to buy with this year's bonus" (for a time there was even a magazine in the UK called *Stuff* devoted entirely to boys' toys – the latest gadgets and stylish tools for the hip new executive)? Whereas *Cosmopolitan* in the seventies educated and liberated its female readership with information on how to produce a bigger and better orgasm, now in the nineties the men's magazines gave advice on how to deal with office politics, how to have the perfect office romance, and how to get a decent raise. Meanwhile, *Fast Company* carried features and advertising aimed at giving people guidance on what to wear in this post-suit, dressed-down world of the new economy.

Having led both the dotcom boom and the rediscovery of work as cool, however, the US, stung by economic downturn and the return of layoffs and the specter of recession, began to look more soberly at the issue of life and work. Yes, we were now able to talk freely about work/life balance, about organizations which truly valued their people, even about ambition and hard work bringing unimagined wealth. (The eighties had been the "greed is good" decade, but in the nineties you could get rich and not be seen as greedy – the money you got being a clear and obvious reward for talent and hard work rather than the result of predatory company asset-stripping or avaricious junk bond trades.)

But there were downsides. Work seemed suddenly to be so cool that we were doing it every hour we could. "First mover" – getting your product to market before your competitors could – became the guiding principle in new economy companies. Working weeks of 80/90/100 hours were common in garages and incubators across the world. (Note how even the language being used fed the cult(ure) of revolution. The "office as garage" where a new generation of Bill Hewletts and Dave Packards might in secret be changing the entire world. Or workplaces where rare and special talent was being "incubated" in laboratory conditions away from the distractions of the world outside. Such metaphors fed not only the atmosphere of revolution but also the need for extreme sacrifice in terms of hours worked.) Meanwhile in the "old economy" organizations, which had stripped themselves lean to the bone through a decade of downsizing and re-engineering, long hours were also common simply because there were fewer people around but more work to do. More information rushing around the world equates to more opportunities to take, more decisions to make, smarter customers to satisfy. The advance of communication technologies and the globalization of businesses pushed us towards an always on, 24/7 society. The working breakfast, the no-alcohol lunch (if lunch at all) and the networking dinner all became part of this pervasive "work hard, work long" ethic.

In August 2000, Tina Brown's *Talk* magazine saw both good and bad in the new cool of work. For them, the most significant symptom of the "new Puritanism" was what they termed "anhedonia" – the inability to find pleasure to leisure. People were finding it difficult to be satisfied with what they had because "we're too busy fretting about what we've yet to achieve."

Certainly, the magazine admitted, our leisure hours had become more stressful and more focused on being productive rather than being simply restful or purely pleasurable. We leave the office and go the gym (if need be, we find a 24-hour gym so that we can still do the 15-hour day at the office and then tend to our physical fitness). We order our children's play time so that it is educational. We work on the house – DIYing like never before spurred on by whole new TV channels devoted to home improvements – to make it a better financial investment. No surprise then that in the UK at least, psychologists have identified something called "weekend stress" ("Oh God, it's Saturday morning, I've got to go and watch Johnny playing soccer, I've got to visit the Mother, I've got to get to Home Depot on the way back . . .").

So it goes without saying that we are living in very interesting times when it comes to the subject of work and life.

So how does this title try to make sense of what is going on in life and work?

In this title, *Life and Work Express*, we'll be looking at three intertwined strands:

1. *Life and Work Express* is an enquiry into the relationship of work to life. It looks at questions such as "what is work for?" and "what role does it play in your life?"

The commonly accepted wisdom is that most people want two things from their work. They want some rewards (essentially financial reward, money, cash, moolah, dosh, dough, spondoolicks, the readies, show me the money man, show me the money) and they want some job satisfaction. Actually the commonly accepted wisdom is that people really want the rewards most of all, and they'll take whatever satisfaction they can get as a nice bonus (but maybe a cash bonus is better). But still others look at work entirely differently, seeing the work you do as not only an expression of your talents but as a revelation of your essential purpose and personal vision: in other words, an answer to the big question "why am I here?". In *Life and Work Express* we'll be looking at all sides of the enquiry. As the intensification of work and the consequent fragmentation of home life continues, what might work be for a healthy individual in a healthy society?

2. It's about the balance between life and work – and what organizations and individuals can do to achieve it

As Nordstrom and Ridderstralle point out in their hugely successful book *Funky Business* (and go and see these two Prada-wearing hipper-than-hip Stockholm professors presenting live if you are still unconvinced that business has become the new rock and roll), Marx was right: the workers now do own the means of production. It is human knowledge, ideas and creativity, rather than sweat-producing manual labor, which makes a company unique and valuable. Talent makes capital dance. And so organizations have been working hard over the last five years to make themselves as attractive as possible to the best (and therefore scarcest) talent. And they have been working hard to help their employees live balanced lives, on the understanding that if you're a happy employee, you'll stay at my company and not go off to my competitors.

So what are the best companies doing to prove the statements they make in their annual reports: that people are their greatest assets?

3. *Life and Work Express* is about taking responsibility for your working effectively by managing yourself better

No matter how you think after the enquiry of strand (i) above – *what role does work play in your life?* – it will almost always be true among readers of this title that you'll invest more time in your work than you do in your personal, non-work life. Because of this, and because for most of us work brings greater financial, material and psychological rewards (in the form of promotion, raises or job satisfaction) the better we execute it, *Life and Work Express* will look at some of the ways we can become more effective at the doing of our work.

For a more thorough examination of this strand, however, I point you to the nine other titles in this Exec Express module:

» *Working Globally*
» *Career Management*
» *Travel*
» *Flexible and Virtual Working*
» *Lifelong Learning*
» *Body Care*
» *Free Agency*
» *Time Management*; and
» *Stress Management.*

In this age of Me Plc, Brand of You and Unit of One, we look at ways that all of us can take more responsibility for the effectiveness of our working lives.

SUMMARY

» A global and technological revolution has changed the way business is done – and the way people think about work.
» The talent of the individual – the "unit of one" – rather than the might of the institution is the new source of power.
» Speed, skill and daring characterize this powershift, a revolution against the status quo.
» Work becomes the new cool – but so do pressures to work harder and longer.
» Individuals need to take responsibility for their own careers in three main areas:

» how they think about work; the role it plays in their lives;
» the balance between work and personal time;
» the way they manage themselves – almost as a business of one (Me Plc).

Evolution of Life and Work

How have we got to where we are in our considerations of life and work? Chapter 3 reviews the evolution of work as a human activity, the rise of management as a practice and a philosophy:

» out of Eden and into labour
» the rise of the gurus
» the results of global change: New Labour?

OUT OF EDEN AND INTO LABOR

Work is one of those things that very obviously proves the idea that how you think about something creates its reality. Show me a person who believes that an organization is a faceless, pre-determined set of structures and processes and I'll show you a person who finds it profoundly difficult to change – or even commit to the possibility of change. Show me a person who believes that work is a form of punishment and slavery and I'll show you a person who struggles to draw any real pleasure or sense of purpose from their work, no matter what they try.

Compare that to the maid who is cleaning my hotel room as I write this very paragraph, the one who is singing and smiling, sharing jokes with her colleague, moving with energy and focus around the series of distinct tasks which she no doubt does every single day and which are no doubt detailed somewhere by the hotel management in a manual entitled *Effective Room Cleansing Process* – and I'll be able to remind you that even the most mundane (and poorly paid) of tasks can be infused with meaning and even – come on, let's use the word – fun.

So if the way we think about work goes a large way towards determining our experience of it, it might be useful to examine where we get our ways of thinking from.

In the Book of Genesis, God is very specific about what work is for. Work is a punishment for having eaten of the tree of knowledge. The serpent tempts Eve, Eve tempts Adam, all hell breaks loose, and before we know it, we are all doomed like Adam:

> "Cursed is the ground because of you; through painful toil you will eat of it all the days of your life ... until you return to the ground ... for dust you are, and to dust you will return."

Painful toil. So if the thought of another Monday morning at work fills you with dread, take my advice, leave your boss alone. Blame the serpent.

[Things, of course, were doubly bad for Eve, who apart from the toil thing, was condemned to the pains of childbearing (named by God, with delicious irony I think, "labor").]

So one thing is clear: the evolution of our own work is in how we think about it. That should be a reassuring principle, since it admits that in even the dullest work and in the most trying circumstances, the possibility of transformation. What really needs to be examined, however, is not just our attitude to the work we happen to be doing at any one point – but our attitude to work itself. Because if we're actually still believing the Genesis story of work-as-punishment, we won't ever find a job that nurtures our life.

But what are the historical origins of work and how has work changed over the centuries? That is another story.

I HAVE IN MY HAND A LUMP OF FLINT

We know from archaeological work carried out in Tanzania that mankind had learnt to use rudimentary tools as far back as 2.5 million years ago. What did they do with those tools? Obviously, they hunted. But did they all hunt, and all the time? No. The anthropologist Richard Lee, who spent fifteen months living with the Kalahari bushmen, found that the adults would spend no more than two or three days a week looking for food. That leaves a long weekend of talking and dancing. Something else they did with the tools, of course, was make other tools, and, as Richard Donkin suggests in his examination of work, *Blood, Sweat and Tears*, it is not too fanciful to suggest that tool making was an art only mastered by those few who developed a particular expertise in it.

They must have made tools on behalf of others; their time and talent must have had some value. Was there some form of trade to acknowledge this? Perhaps the cave painters were specialists too, and released from other duties to carry out their "work." (In which case, work already had an inherent value – before any economic one – based on it being a manifestation of talent and something worthy of both pride and respect.)

There are other things that early man learnt to do with his tools. First, he learnt to make machines that would enable him to satisfy his basic need for food. The grindstone mill is an example of this, a huge technological breakthrough of immense and universal benefit, but which brought with it another learning: that there are some tasks that we'd choose not to do if we had the choice – that there are some activities which we'd much prefer others to do on our behalf. Like turning the grindstone, for example. And this in turn brings us to the next use of the tool: to make weapons. And here we have a marvelous solution to the problem of those niggardly but important little jobs that we'd prefer not to do ourselves: go out, conquer a tribe, and put them to work on the grindstone. The grindstone can be dated back almost 50,000 years. And that's where the daily grind of work began. Here work gains its sense – which many of us feel every day – that it is a series of activities to be avoided by those who are privileged (by money, status or power) to do so.

For the greatest early civilizations, Egypt, Greece, Rome, enslaving people to their work was the way they ensured the ascendancy of their empires over the rest of the world (and how they built the pyramids, of course). But the work-as-slavery metaphor carries itself through to the modern day for many people in how they think about their worklives.

Lotteries all over the world promise a release from *having to work* (it's usually the first thing the media asks the latest multi-millionaire: "will you be going back to work on Monday?"; the biggest fantasy we have, perhaps, is what we'd say to the boss were we to be the lucky one at this week's draw). But very, very, few human beings are forced to work – in the sense in which slaves are subjugated by compulsion and threat to their labors. For the vast majority of us, what we do every day is a choice we make, the self-direction of which has become obscured by habit. If we didn't work, of course, we wouldn't be able to pay the mortgage and feed the children. But even those obligations we choose freely to make.

Freedom as opposed to coercion and slavery is a common metaphor in modern management theory. In other titles in this *Life and Work* series, such as *Travel, Flexible & Virtual Working* and, of course, *Free Agency*, you'll be able to see how organizations, enabled by the latest technologies, are attempting to free people from the constrictions of having to work in the same office every day – so work as something we do rather than a place we go. "Empowerment" was the biggest management fad of the early nineties – the practice of devolving authority and responsibility for task and process down the hierarchy; in manufacturing companies to the factory floor and in service businesses to the customer-facing frontline.

Henry Ford famously regretted that every time he hired a pair of hands for his automobile assembly line, it unfortunately had to come accompanied by a human mind too, but now so much work is the work of knowledge and ideas and relationship that organizations are concerned not to enslave their staff but to release their fullest potential.

A NEW WAY OF THINKING

Until the fifteenth century, Roman Catholicism was both the primary religion of Western Europe and the most potent example of organizational power. The Church – ruling England through the throne but with the backing of God and The Pope in Rome – controlled people's intellectual and spiritual lives through its teachings, but importantly also their domestic life through estate management and the feudal system. Resentment festered for centuries, revolt was inevitable. And when it came, in the form of the Protestant Reformation, it ushered in an entirely different attitude towards economics.

The excess and pride of the Roman Church was to be replaced by a code of ethics which extoled the virtues of industry and thrift. Thus was introduced to the minds of Europeans – and in time to those in the US – the Puritan work ethic. Look at some dealer making markets solidly through the day, fueled by ambition and coke; look at some programmer crafting a piece of software beauty through the night, fueled by ambition and cold pizza, and you'll see the Puritan work ethic in all its glory. Some of us – perhaps many of us – work like our souls, not just our stock options, depend on it, and that's exactly the theological concept. Only work – hard work – will set us free.

A NEW WAY OF DOING

Protestantism valued industry, effort, pragmatics, and practicalities. When Abraham Darby first started forging iron at his works in Ironbridge, England, in the early 1700s, he also sparked the catalyst of a huge shift in the way work was organized – and how work would impact our lives. The new doings made available by human invention and the newish thinkings of Puritan ethics were a perfect match, a match not made in heaven perhaps, but on earth.

Arkwright's spinning jenny, Crompton's mule and Cartwright's power loom, driven by James Watt's advances in steam power, in the burgeoning time of innovation and invention, all helped to make it inevitable that the focus of work would shift from the land and the country to the factory and the city.

The factories that flourished over the next hundred years were based on a systemization of work into jobs, jobs done in shifts, shifts overseen by a hierarchy of management, rewarded by regular wages. None of these elements were new, but their bringing together into the package called *an organisation* was.

All progress has its drawbacks, of course, so the story of the industrial revolution is one of entrepreneurialism and vast fortunes on one hand, and one of drudgery and the fall of the skilled artisan and craftsperson on the other. Mass employment was the dispensation of the new industrialists, and you either were in it, or out of it.

Men worked in the forge and the pit, women and children, often drafted in from the poor houses, in the mills. The biggest part of wages for many of these new workers was paid in food and lodging, and the smallest part in cash, so that workers were obligated to stay with their employers, no matter how harsh the conditions. And conditions were severely harsh, though it could be argued that much of the cruelty was a byproduct of employer ignorance and naivete rather than pure malice. The supervisors of labor, former farm workers themselves, had no management theory to inform them. There would need to be a shift in how people were managed and how the work was done before the employees in these new factories and workplaces could be valued and treated more humanely.

A MORE PRECISE WAY OF DOING

Frederick Taylor was not the inventor of scientific management, but has become most famous – or notorious – for its theory and practice. By the Victorian era, on both sides of the Atlantic, workers often responded to callous mistreatment with secret trade unions, and even sabotage or rioting. Taylor and his predecessors (such as George Pullman, the luxury railroad magnate) hoped that by applying the science of measurement and efficiency conditions would become safer and more pleasant for the worker, the product better for the customer, and the profits higher for the shareholders – though perhaps their instincts were not to look for benefits in that order.

In his observations at the Midvale steel works in Philadelphia from 1880 onwards, Taylor noted that many workers, paid piece-meal, were in fact spending a lot of physical energy and intellectual ingenuity in finding ways to look busy whilst not achieving too much. They had worked out that extra effort did not always, in the dubious and shifting reward structures that management had put in place, equate to higher pay. Thus Taylor's belief that man was essentially an idle worker, and, as time went on, grew a whole industry of motivational theory based on that belief.

By refining the machinery and tools that the workers used, so that the requirement for individual expertise and experience was much reduced, and by obsessively focusing (through the introduction of the stopwatch) on personal productivity, Taylor encouraged the work in factories to become more and more standardized and mechanized. The rewards for entrepreneurs like Henry Ford at his auto plants in Detroit were enormous, particularly when he introduced the moving assembly line, which kept the worker stationary and focused on a single task repeated again and again throughout the day.

The recompense for such mind-numbingly boring labor, to Ford workers at least, came in the form of unprecedentedly high wages. Workers became richer as goods became less expensive. And so it was that efficient factories could deliver better, more varied and cheaper goods to the very same working classes who helped build them. Capitalism gave birth to consumerism. Happiness used to come just through hard work in the days of the Puritans; now it came equally from the stuff that it could buy, buy, buy.

THE RISE OF THE MANAGEMENT GURUS

Taylor was a foreman himself before he became a management theorist. Elton Mayo, on the other hand, was a Harvard Business School professor invited by Western Electric at its Hawthorne plant in 1927, to look for ways to improve the well-being and the output of the workers there.

When they found that improving the lighting improved productivity, they were hardly surprised, but were confused when they found that in some areas output increased when lighting improved. And thus the plunge of managerial theory and practice into the pool of human complexity.

Mayo's conviction was that the odd results of the Hawthorne experiments could be explained thus: the workers improved their work, not because the light made a difference to them, but because, in the moments of those experiments, they were special. They were made to feel important, their work significant. The human relations movement was born, and companies began to consider that they needed not just supervisors with stopwatch and workbook, but counselors with empathy and consideration.

Employees would work for the monetary reward, and the higher the better, but they also wanted to feel part of a community with purpose and humanity. A whole raft of management theorists began exploring not just productivity but also the murky waters of human psychology and motivation. Druker, Deming, Follet, Herzberg, Maslow, McGregor all helped influence thinking on why people work, and how they might do it better. And they were part of an industry which proved that management itself had become both a science and an art. Some of their ideas are explored in Chapter 8: Key Concepts and Thinkers.

One of the leading exponents of the guru industry in the late twentieth century was Dr Michael Hammer, whose business process reengineering brought radical redesigns to organizations and their processes and to great improvements in productivity and profit. What was clear was that reengineering could not manifest its promised benefits without the laying-off of thousands of workers from companies all over the world. A new jargon flourished, perhaps to disguise the pain and distress that reengineering brought to many people's livelihoods. The mid-1990s were the years of downsizing, outsourcing, delayering, and even right-sizing.

It was all very cruel but it brought us a certain set of kindnesses. Never again would organizations be so flabby and overstuffed with workers (at whatever level on the hierarchy) who were not essential to requirements, and who were being rewarded on years of tenure rather than on merit. Making organizations flatter and leaner released many workers as never before to use their own powers of judgement, skill and influencing. It was easier now to see that layers of management slowed decision-making, and brought out some of the darker sides of human behavior, such as doing what it takes to please the boss rather than doing everything possible to please the customer.

These lessons were important ones to learn as the industrial revolution gave way to the information age – and whole new forms of organizing and leading businesses. But the technology revolution brought also whole new experiences of life and work, some of which are only now being hinted at. And that is the focus of the next chapter.

SUMMARY

- » our experience of work is conditioned largely by how we think about it.
- » to examine our assumptions and core beliefs about work, we need to look at its evolution.
- » Genesis tells a story of work as punishment – is this what conditions most of our beliefs of work?
- » early Man made tools and cave paintings – some did these tasks on behalf of others – was this the birth of "work?"
- » the early empire builders used conquest and slavery to separated those tasks that someone else could do on the behalf of those privileged to avoid them – was this the birth of the worker and the manager?
- » the Puritan work ethic promised freedom of the soul through hard labor of the body; the industrial revolution provides ample opportunity for hard labor.
- » Frederick Taylor and a new breed of management gurus designed workplaces around standardization and repetition, devaluing the talent and heart of the worker – a situation twentieth-century management development has been trying to reverse with the advent of the information age and focus on "people as our greatest asset".

The E-Dimension

Here we look at how the Internet and the information age has brought profound changes in how people connect in their lives and work. We will look at the consequences, both good and bad, of living in a world of rapid, disruptive, technological change:

» more mobility
» greater possibilities
» deeper insecurities

So there used to be personnel management, then there came human resources. And now there's E-HR, or so the mailing advertising a new conference tells me:

> "Many in-house corporate activities will be outsourced to different service providers. For example, Morgan Stanley Dean Witter forecasts the market for integrated outsourced HR services will grow from $1 billion in 1999 to $12 billion in 2003."

This is just one example of the rise of connection as a principle and a process.

Global supply chains, heavily dependent on information technology, will grow through joint ventures, strategic alliances and partnerships. Co-operation and relationship will be the principle as well as the practice, and the skills required to manage these alliances will increasingly be those of relationship-building, co-ordination, communication, negotiation, empathy and emotional intelligence.

More and more, for some, our lives at work will be based around activities that increase the range and depth of connections, which is good news for us all, since the human being is nothing if not a social being. People are desperate in these fragmented times for connection – to each other, to themselves, to a cause or purpose. Organizations are desperate to connect employee to employee, employee to supplier, and employee to customer. The Internet makes this range of connections a reality and the work that the Internet enables delivers the activities and behaviors of relationship-making which individuals so value. The worldwide Web is both a product and symbol of human need to share, to come together, to connect.

Or at least this will be the case for the educated, connected ones – people like you. You will be required to become physically, emotionally and psychologically mobile as you travel from project to project, connecting temporarily to one set of people and one set of objectives, and disconnecting as easily as you unplug your laptop. But you'll be highly paid for your talents and your pains. Your workplaces, if they are not home, may look more like hotels and clubs than the office-factories of the last generation.

For low-paid occupations such as receptionists, cleaners, ticket collectors and the employees of call centers (the new sweatshops), things will be a lot slower to change. They'll still commute every day, to do the same work, in the same building, surrounded by the same people. And they may not be always happy with their lot.

Robert M. Worcester, the chairman of the research organisation MORI, suggests that there are some worrying downsides to the e-revolution, and lists a series of resentments building up as the information age reaches its maturity:

» young against old
» poor against rich
» rural against urban
» scientists against the people
» producers against the consumers
» people against the institutions
» central government against local government
» everybody against big business
» the globalized (many) against the globalizers (few).

He identifies one way in which these resentments will surface. Thirty-eight percent of us, apparently, have told MORI that we have taken positive action of some sort to shun companies who offend our sense of ethics and values (i.e., by purchasing from their more ethically healthy competitors).These are rational, responsible, non-violent ways of behaving.

Francis Fukuyama, however, is less optimistic that these are the only behavioral outputs of the e-revolution. In his *The Great Disruption: Human Nature and the Reconstitution of Social Order*, Fukuyama questions the almost universally positive celebration of the information age which has been the fashion ever since the futurist Alvin Toffler in 1980 termed it *the third wave*, and described it as significant a shift in human history from the two previous "waves" – from hunter-gatherer to agricultural societies, and from agricultural societies to industrial ones. Fukuyama's powerful and data-rich work signals a seemingly undeniable truth: that "with all the blessings that flow from a more complex, information-based economy, certain bad things also happened to our social and moral life."

Unfortunately, the good is intertwined with the bad. Increased information tends to produce, or at least promise, what most people want: freedom and equality. This leads to the hundred or so channels on your TV set, but also to the delayering of the large bureaucracies as they empower their people with more and more information. This is true of IBM and AT&T and it is true of the former Soviet Union and Eastern Germany. Unfortunately, the rise of individualism – the unit of one, the be anything you want to be, the just do it, the you can have it all creeds – brings a consequent disabling of the bonds that link families, communities and nations together. Here's one extremely simplified example: the more women in a society who work in organizations and follow their own careers, the more that society's understanding of what constitutes a family – and indeed whether families are important – is corroded.

What worries Fukuyama is how the message of individualism is cloaked in the language and energy of rebellion, of non-conformism, of the liberation movement (compare *Fast Company*):

> "The 'no-limits' message is, then, a problematic one. We want to break rules that are unjust, unfair, irrelevant or outdated, and we seek to maximize personal freedom. But we also need new rules to permit new forms of co-operative endeavour and to enable us to feel connected with one another in communities. These new rules always entail the limitation of individual freedom ... The same society that wants 'no-limits' to its technological innovation also sees 'no-limits' to many forms of personal behavior, and the consequent growth of crime, broken families, parents failing to fulfil obligations to children, neighbors not looking our for each other, and citizens opting out of public life."

Similarly, Paul Edwards at the Henley Centre is unsure how people's behavior will be affected by the inherent insecurities that are the consequence of living in a world of rapid, disruptive, technological change. He gives the example of research his organization has undertaken which shows that less than a quarter of consumers have confidence that they'll be making the right decision when making a complicated and expensive product, such as a car or a pension. Increased choice is not always a pleasant thing.

He describes the sensation of being both in and out of control as being an increasingly prevalent one for many people. They have a huge amount of autonomy, talent and money and also a huge amount of insecurity and instability in their employment, their family and social lives and in their relationships with institutions such as church and government. In and out of control; it's a crazy rollercoaster ride.

People will need to draw deep from inside themselves as they manage their lives and work through these disturbances. How many of us will have sufficient reserves of energy and confidence?

For many of us, for the time being, the most disruptive yet prosaic impact of the e-revolution on our lives and work is in the form of information overload. E-mail and voice-mail were supposed to allow us to communicate faster, thus freeing our time up for the important stuff like work. Ha! If they built more roads, they also thought, naively, there'd be more space between cars, making driving a more pleasurable, effective and ecologically clean activity. Unfortunately, the use of cars increased to clog the newer, wider roads, no matter how many they built. So too with the information superhighway. Suddenly, says Richard Donkin in *Blood Sweat and Tears*, "information was spinning into our laps like junk mail, like discarded litter. This wasn't information but information pollution . . . Work? The chance would be a fine thing."

E-mail is a fascinating medium because it is so rich in its implications. From one perspective, its simplicity is wondrous. But e-mail's simplicity is also its poisoned chalice. The uses and abuses of it allow us to consider behaviors such as power-playing (who do you *cc* and who not?); ass-covering (why do you *cc*?); withdrawing (when do you use the *Out of Office* feature?); self-aggrandisement (how often do you log on a day?) – and the role of the culture of the organization in allowing or discouraging these behaviors.

But there are even darker sides to the rise of the Internet – and technology more generally – when it comes to the subject of life and work. Four come to mind here.

THE ALWAYS ON EXECUTIVE

All those cell-phones, pagers, laptops and pda devices which we're so terrified of leaving behind on the train in the morning are inextricably linked to the darker excesses of work and life. They make routine tasks easier and they lower the costs of business – unquestionably. Without doubt, they also increase business performance through optimising personal productivity – but there is a cost. They push us towards an always-on, always-connected existence. We can be always in touch – whether in the plane, in our hotel room, commuting home – so physically being out of the office is no longer the problem it was. We take our work and our workloads with us.

So where is work, and when does the working day end? How can we leave it all behind, as stress and time management courses used to teach us? Where does personal time begin – and what happened to the concept of "down time?" Even the necessary evil of corporate travel used to have an accompanying benefit – that at least you could be on your own for a while. How many of us have the confidence, the nerve, to turn off that cellphone and go and sit in the new Quiet Carriages that are springing up on the UK's commuter rail network?

THE PHYSICAL DISCOMFORTS OF NEW TECHNOLOGY

And they're heavy, all those lumps of metal and plastic. Watch that hassled executive lugging his computer bag and wheelie case across the airport and I'll show you the strains on his occipital. Your mobile phone emits radiation and cooks your brain, whilst your computer gets you three ways. It gives you back strain from the way you sit at the desk to operate it, gives you wrist strain from tapping away at its keyboard too long and gives you eye strain from staring at it all day. They all give you a headache when they fail to work. And why – because you're scared of what you'll miss whilst not connected ... (or scared that if you can't keep checking messages now, that'll mean a landslide of unattended mail when finally you do get back "on line").

THE SPY IN THE MACHINE

Frederick Taylor stood over the employees he was scrutinizing with a stopwatch to look for minute improvements in what they did. He'd have had an easier time of it in the early twenty-first century.

In her book *White-Collar Sweatshop*, Jill Andresky Fraser outlines some wonderful new devices for "monitoring and controlling the work-place". She talks, for example, about the " *Investigator*" programme, sold by WinWhatWhere Corporation, which can be installed by a company on any or all of its desktop computers to record how many keys were stroked, mouses clicked and commands entered by employees during a given day. As Fraser points out, such tools are not always going to be used as productivity-boons. One company's knowledge management software is another's *big brother*. " *Investigator"* can be programmed so that whenever an "alert" word or phrase is typed, the document in which it is being used is automatically e-mailed to the appropriate supervisor. Be afraid. Or be aware. But whatever, just be careful about writing "My boss is a fat warthog" or "I'm starting a union – join up today!"

The American Management Association, by the way, estimated that, by 1999, 67 percent of American companies were monitoring their employees' e-mails, or otherwise checking up on them through video surveillance, phone-call tracking, electronic monitoring of computer work and so on.

A PLACE TO BE DISGRUNTLED

Those who were brave or foolhardy enough to keep telling whoever would listen how much they hated their work found the Internet to be a great place to build their very own community. If you can't find enough people in your own company to whinge with at the watercooler, get on line and share your tales of woe with a whole bunch of other disaffected workers.

Or so seemed to be the message of a number of anti-work, anti-corporate or "worker-support" sites that have grown over the last five years. Some have a seemingly beneficial mission: bullybusters.com is run by the *Campaign against Workplace Bullying* and offers research, education and "help and solutions". Others such as insiderviews.com support a cause: issues relating to the treatment of women in the workplace. Still others seem to have little use other than to convince its visitors that the grass is never greener on the other side.

Jobhater.com offers *Revenge Story of the Week* and *Best Stupid Boss Quotes*. Here's an example from the site: "The boss and his wife (the real boss) had bought this old HP fax machine and he would claim that he was the only one that could fix the damn thing. It would jam every day and beep really loud when it stopped working. One day I decided to send faxes endlessly when I was at home, just to see how annoyed they would get. Sure enough they bought a new one the next day."

Disgruntled.com was a sharp monthly Internet magazine dedicated to the dysfunctional workplaces suffered by A. Nonymous and the like all over the US. Its creator, Daniel S. Levine, sold t-shirts as well as advertising, and then wrote the "book of the site" (average five-star rating on amazon.com!) The magazine folded in 2000, but there was still time for a last laugh from the editor. As the home page now reads:

> "We are sorry to report that 'Disgruntled' editor Daniel S. Levine has resigned because of an ongoing dispute over wages, benefits and working conditions at this magazine. As a result, we are ceasing publication until such time that we can resolve the matter."

Clearly a man who didn't find his own work to be unabashed misery and despair, then. . .

Vault.com is an upmarket site described as the insider career network, and offers a range of services from recruitment to coaching to litigation advice. It is often read by those who are thinking about joining a new company, because the site has in depth information about thousands of organisations, including a Message Board service where current employees can tell anyone who is interested what it's really like to work at the company in question. Some of the (again anonymous) entries reveal how deeply some people are affected by their work (and how unbalanced they can become in the process):

> "At training, the firm spent thousands to write a pathetic theme song [for the company]. (I guess HR has to justify their useless existence somehow.)
> While driving home after another 14-hour day, the song "Rape Me" by Nirvana [sic] came on the radio. This should be the theme for our firm.
> It is exactly how the staff is treated. This place will abuse you, make you give up almost everything in your personal life, and then cast you aside."

But then they probably said that about Frederick Taylor and his stopwatch too...

SUMMARY

» global supply chains, heavily dependent on information technology, will grow through joint ventures, strategic alliances and partnerships.

» the skills required to manage these alliances will increasingly be those of relationship-building, co-ordination, communication, negotiation, empathy and emotional intelligence.

» there may be an increasing gap – and conflict – between those who have these skills and these jobs and those who continue to carry out necessary but "mundane" tasks.

» we will all be affected by the inherent insecurities that are the consequence of living in a world of rapid, disruptive, technological change.

» major symptoms so far include:

  » information overload;

  » the 24/7, "always-on" expectation;

  » physical discomforts produced by new technologies;

  » the hi-tech monitoring by employers of staff activity.

The Global Dimension

Your life at work may be as part of a global organization; even as a free agent you're only a click away from new learning or opportunities worldwide. This chapter investigates some of the key considerations behind seeing oneself as a world citizen:

» transnational mega-powers – the pros and cons
» implications for individuals' behavior

"There is a new form of global competition. Companies all over the world are competing with each other to become known as the best employer in their industry or community. This is a most welcome development – with profound implications, not only for the business world, but for society as a whole."

Richard Levering, compiler of The 100 Best Companies to Work for in America *list*

In every industry, companies face more competition than ever before. This is true even in industries that were previously thought to be totally secure. In the United States, industries such as airlines, electric utilities and telecommunications have been deregulated. The competition is global. Competitors can appear from anywhere, and they do. Size and place do not have a constraining hold on success. There has been the death of distance. Small software companies in Australia can and do gain contracts with large companies in Arizona in the US. They are competing with similar software houses in Australia, Arizona and, for that matter, Altrincham, UK. Although they are clearly competing for business, they are also competing for the available talent – and for the hearts and minds of their customers. Globalization brings a worldwide stage for companies to parade their worklife initiatives, their internal as well as their external brands.

It brings also a whole new arena for being found out: the lights shone on companies on the global stage have a tendency to make them transparent. People can find out about Nike's questionable employment practices very quickly – and equally as quickly they can communicate their findings around the world. Some of those people will want to take action. This is the age not just of the smarter, more demanding customer, but the activist consumer too. One in six of us has already boycotted a company's product on ethical grounds. One in five of us has positively chosen a product or service because of a company's ethical standpoint (Data from Mori). But boycotting products is not all some people want to do, as we have seen recently in Genoa and Seattle.

The first transnational corporations were the Roman Empire and the Church. So megacompanies with a global reach are not exactly new. But the global companies of today raise some profound ethical considerations, not least to do with the use of power and size.

Just the week before I delivered this title to the publishers, *The Independent Magazine* ran a feature on a new book called *Trade* (published in September by Fotomuseum Winterthur & Scalo and distributed by Thames and Hodder). *Trade* is a book of photographs interspersed with text from philosophers, economists and social commentators, looking at multiple manifestations of commerce in our age. It looks a spooky book. One of the most striking images is a simple photograph of the Nestle boardroom; large table, twenty-two chairs, one wall taken up with a giant map of the world, as if from an old Bond villain's lair – but no human beings in the shot at all.

Trade's message seems to be that whether we are cruising a mall or a red light district, we are all buying and selling – and, by implication, being bought and sold. The authors have a point. You can put your resume on a global website, and go to work wherever they'll have you, if you're flexible and talented enough. On another website, you might put your partner's nude shots – someone, somewhere, will pay something for them. Indeed, an interesting side effect of the global, Internet economy is the rise of "amateur" pornography, a combination perhaps not just of our individual exhibitionist tendencies but our commercial ones as well. We can all be standardized, commoditized and branded, whatever our work.

But back to those big companies. As Bruce Nixon points out in *Global Forces*, the turnover of General Motors, Ford, Exxon and Shell exceeds that of the whole of Africa. Microsoft is wealthier than Switzerland. [More data: Four hundred and fifty billionaires have a combined wealth of £860 billion, which is equivalent to the wealth of 45 percent of the world's population and more than the GNP of China.]

Good for them of course, but these corporations do not operate in a vacuum. The global economy connects them very solidly to the world. At one end of the spectrum, they have a profound impact on the global ecology, and do so largely unchecked by governments. As George Soros says in *The Crisis of Global Capitalism*:

"the basic unit of political and social life remains the nation state ... ecological threats are not adequately dealt with ... global financial markets are largely beyond the control of national or international authorities ... the current state of affairs is unsound and unsustainable."

At the other end of the spectrum, these mega-companies are connected to the individuals who populate the Filipino shanty towns, the Ukranian clochards, and the poverty-stricken villages of India and Africa, because that's where – and by whom – their "exports" are "processed."

The current fashion is for activism and protest, yet the prevailing mood is one of confusion and uncertainty, a rebellion without a real cause. As *The Independent* piece remembers, one protester in London unfurled a banner reading "Smash Capitalism and Replace it With Something Nice." These are unusual protests, a topsy turvy spin on a generation ago when penniless hippies proclaimed that all we needed was love. Now, it seems, we have the money, but lack the vision.

How will all this affect you? Some of you will join the protests against capitalism. The available data – and the images on the Internet – which detail the growing gap between the rich and poor of the world is quite liable to provoke moral outrage. Many of you will direct your energies behind "the sustainability movement" against the damaging impacts of global trade on the environment, on indigenous lifestyles, and on the health of individuals. (Data showing different perspectives on the same issue: an estimated 24,000 people in the UK alone dies prematurely because of pollution; 5000 people a week decide to become vegetarian...)

Some of you will focus your distrust not on capitalism in general but institutions in particular. For many, companies may no longer mean what they used to mean to my father:

"... the people who don't have access to a corporation to which they can offer lifelong loyalty are the majority. And for young workers, consistently over-represented among the unemployed, part-time and temporary sectors, the relationship to the work world is even more tenuous...

"Because young people tend not to see the place where they work as an extension of their souls, they have, in some cases, found freedom in knowing they will never suffer the kinds of heart-wrenching betrayals their parents did. For almost everyone who has entered the job market in the last decade, unemployment is a known quantity, as is self-generated and erratic work. In addition, losing one's job seems much less frightening when getting it seemed an accident in the first place. We begin to wonder . . . why we should depend on the twists and turns of large institutions for our sense of self."

Naomi Klein, No Logo

Others will home in on the sense of uncertainty and confusion which appears to be the current, post-boom, edge of global recession zeitgeist:

"When asked what they would be doing in 5 and 10 years, most Generation Xers in a 5-country study found it difficult to answer. Both men and women, particularly the older Generation Xers, said they found it difficult to plan because of the general insecurity around employment. Older respondents said, 'I'm ready to have children now, but I won't do it without a secure job.' "

Jean-Marie Martino, Work-Life Initiatives in a Global Context.
Report for The Conference Board

Others among you will see the many upsides, the huge potential for entrepreneurship in a world gone crazy on brands and the promises brands offer. This is the age of Me Plc and Brand You. (See the *Free Agency* title in this Life & Work series. For some more breathless advice, see Tom Peters' Reinventing Work series, in particular *The Brand You Fifty*.) Still others of you will reject the assertion that everything – you, your life – should be considered a business.

One thing will be true for all of us. All that's left, in the end, are the personal boundaries within which we can assert the dignity of our own labor. That is the place where we can make the most difference to our lives and work.

And that's what the next chapter is about.

EXTRACT OF A LETTER TO HER BOSS FROM A GLOBAL CHILD

Remember when they brought in that work/life balance counsellor to the office a couple of months back? She was good, wasn't she? At any rate, she really helped me to think through some things, get some things clear. I don't know if she did the same for you. But it became easier for me to speak about things which I'd always guessed you weren't supposed to talk about. Like just how pressurised and complex my life is. I look around at my friends and those who aren't my friends and we all seem to be trapped in this mentality that says if you're having fun, if you're being successful, if you've got the right clothes and the right gear and know the right clubs then everything's cool. And there's this thin film separating the me that lives and works in that world where everything's just fine – and from that place it is, because from there I've got a great life – and the me that lives and breathes in this world where I'm only just holding myself together. There's the me that's got all the stuff – and this job has allowed me to get lots of good stuff – and the me that knows it's all pretty worthless. I shut the door at night and there's only me, you know. Even when I'm in a relationship, it's easy to think of the boyfriend as just part of the same stuff.

Remember that article you passed round last year – from that magazine, I can't remember its name. Brand of You or Brand You or something. I get it – I do it well enough. But does it always have to be about me, about the individual? Me Inc. What do I have? What do I need? What's my grade? What university did I go to? What salary do I earn? What do I wear? Because after a time, you find yourself thinking who's got what I want? And who else has got something better than me? You can get sucked into this comparison thing. And we do it at the same time as knowing how superficial it is to do it. And how do you think that feels? "Cool, beautiful, clever and self-contained but please don't let me down."

Have you ever read *American Psycho* by Brett Easton Ellis? Pretty fucked up book, in a way. But it's about this guy who's killing all these girls in some disgusting ways, and at the same time he's always preening around; he loves himself. The book has these long sections which are all about what beauty products he puts on his skin in the morning and where he buys his shoes. I guess it's a satire about appearances and reality, you know? Well last week in the weekend paper there was a feature on male grooming – and one of the young guys in there was inspired to start making himself look good by that character in American Psycho. That's so shallow (but he looked good too).

So I shut the door at night and there's only me, as I say. And all the advertising tells me that I can have what I want, be who I want, have it now. I sometimes wonder whether I'm supposed to think that the brands are all I need to know. That the 97 channels on my TV are all I need to have to be entertained and educated. And other times I just feel that I'm surrounded by a pretence of choice.

Why bother to leave the house? The TV and the Web are my friend and family at the end of a remote or a mouse. Lonely Planet is my buddy in a book. And when I do leave the house, I sit alongside all my colleagues at work staring at a computer screen all day (or once a week we gather in the restaurant to watch a Web-broadcast from our esteemed CEO in LA). Or we go to a bar every night and check each other out – with all the headaches and hangovers that ensue from that. That's why I love clubbing. At least there, when you're dancing, you don't actually have to watch anything . . . All this attention we're paying to someone else, something else, somewhere else. It's like watching someone else take a call on the train at night going home – they always seem to have much more fascinating mates on the other end of the line than ours. Do you know what I mean?

I once read someone describing what I'm talking about here a lot better than I am doing now: they said we were in danger of becoming tourists in our own lives. . .

How am I doing? Dunno. Everything's moving so fast, changing so quickly that I lose track of what I'm being compared against. Where am I headed in my work? Dunno. The timeframes are always so short, that we're always just focusing on what's right in front of us. So there's always a buzz around the place – all that energy being expended has got to produce a buzz, right? – but what it all adds up to, I'm really not sure. And I'm even less sure if it makes me feel good any more.

And yet I'm doing well, aren't I – that's a good chunk of money going in the bank every month. I daren't even tell my parents what I earn, they'd be astonished, appalled. Am I doing well? (Posh and Becks are doing better, right?) Everything's always telling me that everything's always possible, everything's always within reach, that I can have everything I can dream. The magazines tell me I can look good from top to toe and I can have the best sex ever. That I can live the movie. My mum tells me what life used to be like in her day, how I've never had it as good. And sometimes that feels more like a very big weight of expectation, rather than a freedom or a release.

Maybe it's because we never get a feeling that we're completing anything at work. We work on the Yaboya.com account, and even though it's a great success, it never feels like we ever got to the end because by the time it does reach some sort of finish line, the original account team are all split up and working on other things by now. How many celebrations for projects were there last year? The only thing I can remember passing the champagne round for was new business wins. Something new to start working on. . .

So, how do I feel about work? Almost OK, almost worthwhile, almost exhilarating. And at the same time, almost out of control, almost crazy, almost overwhelming. How do I feel? Almost fine. And almost disillusioned. Default setting for emotions: faintly miserable.

What a pain I must be sounding. I've just read through all this again and (a) it's not coming out like I intended it would and (b) Jesus, I sound so pathetic! I should cheer up, huh? I've got lots to be happy about. The apartment, the job, the friends (who I love, by the way). But they never taught us how to be happy at university. They just assumed we'd find out for ourselves I suppose.

My Dad has God – he's a CofE supporter – and I have *The Matrix*. He had Patton and *Reach for the Sky* and I've got *Enemy of the State*.

[Adapted from *Corporate Voodoo: Principles for Business Mavericks and Magicians* by David Firth and Rene Carayol. Acknowledgment of inspiration for above to Dr Nick Baylis, research director for younglives.com; research project into the concerns and hopes of people aged 16–25 in the UK today.]

Postscript 1

I was in San Francisco recently and viewed a documentary called *Secrets of Silicon Valley* (directed by Kaufman and Snitow). It was a look at the soft underbelly of the new world of work. "High Tech" is an industry that presents itself as progressive and liberal, yet there are also indications that it has been anti-union and dismissive of some basic workers rights. Not everyone has become mega-rich in this world. One of the interviewees was a temporary worker at a Hewlett-Packard plant on $8 an hour, who organized a petition amongst his co-workers when he found that pay packets were routinely coming up short. He was successful in this campaign, but went too far when he complained about chronic respiratory diseases and bloody noses, which he claimed were being suffered by his fellow workers at the plant. He was fired. [I should note here that HP hotly denied the allegations. Besides, the plant in question has since been relocated to Mexico. Hey, it's a global world.] The worker in question makes an interesting assertion in the program: that attempting to defend oneself against the rampaging globalization of the world may well be the civil rights movement of our age.

Postscript 2

And others defend themselves against the globalization of the world in very extreme ways. . .

"This attack on the US is part of the dark side of globalization. . ."
The Guardian *September 9, 2001*

SUMMARY

» competitors can appear from anywhere, and they do. Size and place do not have the same constraining hold on success.

» the global stage is a very visible one – companies market themselves intensively (both to customers and new employees) but are also watched by smarter, activist consumers in society.

» mega-companies have reached unprecedented size and power – questions remain about how their activities can be controlled or regulated (e.g. their impact on the environment).

» possible responses for the individual:

  » protest (peacefully or otherwise) against perceived abuses of corporate power.

  » distrust of institutions generally – the rise of individualism and the breakdown of social capital.

  » grasp the many opportunities available to the entrepreneurial free agent.

Work on the circle of influence you have most control over – your work and life.

The State of the Art

What are the key issues being faced today by people wrestling the challenge of optimizing their life at work? What does recent research indicate about the near future? And what should you – or your organization – actually do?

Future success means a capable, committed, diverse and flexible work-force that feels in control of its choices, its time and its life in general. Acquisition of core transferable skills – in particular, good interpersonal communication skills as well as skills in IT – will be key. The costs of lack of worklife balance are well documented. Stress can cause ill-health and dysfunctionality. The pressures of the new 24-hour society and a long-hours culture creates personal, commercial and social problems ... change means unprecedented pressure, and unprecedented opportunity. Everyone needs to develop the skills to balance an increasingly complex set of roles and relationships at work and at home.

There is clearly a strong agenda for government, employers, commercial and community organizations to help us develop the new knowledge, understanding and skills.

INDIVIDUALS TAKING CHARGE: LEARNING FOR LIFE

So, how cool was it for you?

Advocates, apologists and evangelists for the new economy – e.g., *Fast Company* readers – have almost convinced themselves that work will never be the same again. There was a two-year (or perhaps more) window where people appeared to be rewarded (nay, hounded) for their talents, to have greater amounts of autonomy on the job, to work together in ever-changing teams and projects, where new intellectual and emotional stimulation was only ever the next project away, where everyone drank extraordinary amounts of coffee all day (thus making a megalith out of Starbucks and a host of other style/culture cafes, where people did work through the night, but it was fun (and not just because of the inflatable boardroom table and the pool table and the upside down jukebox and, hey, do you remember when Microsoft sent that memo round reminding people to wear their shoes when clients came in) and anyway it wasn't like we had a nasty, exploitative boss forcing us to do it, because we were sharing in the wealth. We were going to be rich. I know a guy and his dog who got very rich indeed.

It's an attractive vision, and for some it was a (albeit temporary) reality. Yet it ignores an equally valid reality: that for many, particularly in "old economy" companies, work never really shifted beyond the mundane and the repetitious.

Andrew Ross, professor and director of the *American Studies Program* at New York University and interviewed online at *Fast Company* August 2001, makes an interesting parallel:

"Employees also had greater liberty to manage themselves. In the history of work, there has never been such emotional self-management on the job. By self-management, I mean the degree to which employees accept or reject the idea that the working day can be a mix of work and play, self-application and dreamy idleness. Ultimately, I'm talking about work rhythms and patterns that imitate the way artists traditionally work. When I'm writing, I spend a lot of time just sort of messing around – writing now and again. Play is critical. Most managers haven't yet been able to incorporate creative meandering in a sustainable way."

He's right, of course. Just recently I had a discussion on the theme of imagination with a team in a client company. This organization is not exactly Silicon Valley, but nor would you suspect it – were I to share its name with you – of being a fuddy, duddy old bureaucratic company. Yet even there, with this group of young professionals, the idea that you might be able to spend a reasonable chunk of time dreaming out of the window was laughed out of court: "My boss would kill me!". Some years back, as workplace design was making itself known to the consciousness of leaders, I discussed with another client – a firm of search and selection consultants – their newly appointed "R&R" room, where staff would be encouraged to de-stress, or simply think. "The first one seen in there," said one of my clients in all seriousness, "will be a very brave person indeed."

We tell ourselves such stories to reassure ourselves that we are right to be afraid, right to be wary, right to be reluctant to change. We can't be blamed, can we, when life is so obviously stacked against us? Yet these stories also create a reality – no one thinking that way will go into the R&R room; therefore the R&R room is a failure; thus it was always just an example of management cynicism. Perhaps one of the factors which created that two-year new economy glimpse of work as a celebration of our talents was a bigness on behalf of those dotcom workers – that they were prepared to step out of the old put-upon, "my-boss-exploits-me, I hate my work" thinking. And they were prepared just to go for it.

They were also, I'd imagine, pretty aware that their talent was intimately connected to business results, in ways it must be difficult to be convinced of if you're working for a large, unwieldy hierarchy. How can we be sure that our efforts, howsoever well intentioned, howsoever carried out with integrity, actually made a difference today? It must have been easier to measure the cause and effect, the talent input/result output link in a new economy company.

There's something else too, something else which might illuminate those millions of us in organizations which barely noticed the new economy bubble. And it's to do with leadership and management. In many of the companies celebrated every month in *Fast Companies*, the idea which birthed the company was very close to the leader. It's a familiar story: Entrepreneur has idea. Can't sleep at night, he or she is so excited. Persuades a few mates to put their energies together behind the idea. Gets some financial backing from an investor. Company succeeds (or fails). Everyone moves on to the next idea.

There's not much time in a lifecycle like that for the management to do anything but make it up as they go along. There's no opportunity for long-established cultures and practices from history to reassert themselves in the present – partly because the organization doesn't have a history. There's no chance that people will start "acting" like bosses, because they won't know what to do anyway (there won't be any mentors around to coach them into "proper" managerial behavior). And besides, when you've got a team of talented software developers in front of you, any one of which could walk out today and straight into another job, no one is going to tolerate anyone like you coming over all boss-man.

This is not to suggest that there was no discipline inside new economy companies, nor that there isn't hard-nosed, extremely focused leadership. Just that there was no time for messing around. There were no text books to study and follow by rote. As Andrew Ross suggests, "these were Renaissance men and women."

The downside, of course, was that the lack of managerial experience was in many ways the cause of the bursting of the dotcom bubble. What we somehow need to cultivate in the healthiest organizations – new or old economy – is the sort of manager who has the wisdom to direct action, without it being accompanied by the sort of arrogant behavior which stifles creativity and dialogue.

When all is said and done, one of the most powerful realizations to come from the dotcom explosion and the " world of work" movement that surrounded it, is one which transcends distinctions such as "new" or "old" economy. What is universally true, what has always been true, is that you can master your own destiny by the application of your talent and influence and by expanding your capacity for change. In the end, it is not the duty of our workplaces to make us happy, or satisfied, or even secure. These are responsibilities we ultimately take for ourselves – or powers we give away if we choose to.

Work and life: some new understandings

Balanced by all that globalization, the standardization, the branding and commodification of everything is a counter philosophy that places the individual at its pinnacle. These are people-centered times. My bookshelf – and I like to think that my bookshelf is reflective of what is most current and cutting edge in the world of work and life – has titles such as the following:

» *Dialogue: the art of thinking together*
» *Bringing Your Soul to Work*
» *The Art of Possibility: transforming professional and personal life*
» *Living Strategy: putting people at the heart of corporate purpose*
» *The Soul at Work: unleashing the power of complexity science for business success*
» *Whole Scale Change: unleashing the magic in organizations*
» *A Simpler Way* (a book about "preserving the color and texture of a vital individual life while joining together to work with others")

What I believe all these books have in common is an understanding that the homo sapiens cannot and need not be separated from homo organizationius. Work is, always is, about people, and so we need to understand ourselves and each other in ever more profound ways. Yet there is also an inference to be drawn from all these books, particularly those which are drawing more and more on the new science discoveries regarding complexity theory, coherence and emergence: that when we study work (or the organization of work) we are in fact studying life itself.

If, as the new sciences suggest, life is always moving towards self-organization, then can we imagine and bring into being organizations which are an affirmation of life itself? It seems an astonishing claim. The old Newtonian/Darwinian understanding of life as a series of mechanical interactions, and organizations as soul-less machines, makes it a lot simpler to blame the machine's originator: the boss. And as soon as we get into blame of bosses, we are trapped in the history of work as enslavement, which spans from *Genesis* to Frederick Taylor. It would be good to consider some new thinking that would allow us to step out of that self-reinforcing cycle.

But if the boss isn't actually in control, if all a boss can really do is nudge at a system and then sit back and see what happens, that means that we ourselves are equally as powerful (and as powerless) as our bosses. Such "living, adaptive systems" would require us all to be more confident, more creative and playful, better at empathy, more forgiving and compassionate when unexpected consequences arose, less judgmental of intentions and efforts; in short, more humane than we currently allow ourselves to be in organizations. These human qualities, perhaps, are the ones we want to express in our private lives. But perhaps it's difficult to turn them on again, like a mechanical switch, if we've turned them off when we go to work. Off, on, off, on. No wonder we're all so tired and disillusioned. But even the contemplation, say, of *A Simpler Way* is a step in the right direction, if it opens up new understanding and responsibilities.

We won't be able to open these things up, however, unless we examine some current paradoxes surrounding the way we work.

The puzzle

As David Blanchflower (Dartmouth College, US) and Andrew Oswald (Warwick University, UK) point out in their June 2000 report *Is Something Wrong with Work-Life Balance? A Look at International Data*:

> "working hours have been trending down steadily for the last century; hence a look at the historical data makes one doubt the thesis that western society is going to hell in a hand-basket of

over-work ... [and] ... as shown in some of our earlier research, people say they enjoy their jobs enormously. Reported degrees of satisfaction at work in the industrialized countries are actually impressively high.''

And yet 85 percent of Americans want more time with their family, and 46 percent say they want much more (in the UK, 36 percent want much more). These are the same people – and it's probably you and me both – who work at a pace and intensity which leaves us both drained and astonished. How can we be doing this to ourselves – and why don't we grant ourselves what we say what we want so much and buy, with all the riches we are accumulating, some time off.

But we don't. "It's a puzzle," say Blanchflower and Oswald. Why does this situation exist?

There are three reasons that I can suggest:

» The situation exists because we're lying to the researchers. I call it *The Little Secret*: that in fact, deep down, many people actually prefer their workplace to their homelife. In the workplace, there's control, respect, help. It's fun or it's dull but it's rarely threatening or even difficult. Not so homelife, with its domestic upheavals and relationship minefields.

» The situation exists because it's a classic prisoner's dilemma, as Blanchflower and Oswald themselves suggest:

"where everyone is behaving rationally individually but as a collective group we are working inefficiently hard. On this view, the group is collectively trapped in a spiral. Keeping up with the Joneses is what rules. In other words, if you work hard, I feel I have to in order to be able to keep up – in chances of promotion at work, in buying the latest cars and sweaters, in simply being seen to be industrious by my neighbors. If we could all agree to slow down together, we could all be happier. Coordinating it is then the tricky bit.''

» The situation exists because work is so consuming, so central a part of our lives, that we become addicted to it. Away from the office, we're terrified of missing something, terrified of being left behind.

It's not so much fear of not getting what others are getting, not being in on what they're in on (as in the prisoner's dilemma idea above). What we're scared of, as addicts always are, is not getting our fix and, more accurately, not being able to stand up to life without that fix.

Obsession: the shadow side of work

I read just last week of a hotel in LA which has a desk situated in the shallow end of one of its swimming pools. The manager reports it "continuously used." Or maybe I dreamt that I read it. Surely such a thing would be the sign of a society going mad on work . . . Someone please tell me that I didn't read that. . .

In London, I pick up a *Daily Telegraph* to find a piece entitled "Hell is getting away from it all" (*Daily Telegraph*, August 28, 2001), about men (and apparently it is usually men), who cut short their vacations because they have an obsessive attachment to work. There are at least two interconnecting threads here. One is that men find it easier to self-aggrandize themselves – to condition themselves to thinking that if they are not there, physically present in their workplace, then bad things will happen. The second thread is the equally dark psychological trait of paranoia – that whilst you're sunning yourself on the beach, your boss is having all your belongings dumped into a black bin liner.

This paranoia has a certain amount of validity for some people, apparently. The piece reports one project manager who returned from vacation to find his desk in the parking space. Just because you're paranoid doesn't mean that they're not out to get you, of course, but whenever I read urban-myth-like stories such as this, I always think that the victims, far from being hapless victims of a brutal regime, must have been deaf, blind and dumb not to read the portents whilst actually in the office before the vacation.

And yet, that's what we do when it comes to work. These stories comfort us, excuse us of the need to be different from the tribe. They encourage us to give our personal power away to some faceless institution and its capricious, amoral bosses. "Our greatest fear is not that we are inadequate" – writes Marianne Williamson in a poem made famous when Nelson Mandela read it at his inaugural speech as South African prime minister – "Our greatest fear is that we are powerful beyond measure."

And so we make ourselves slaves to work when we could be free, bullied when we could be shapers, dumb when we could be influential, victims when we could be co-creators or leaders. The trouble is, the stories of corrupt organizations and evil bosses are tremendously comforting – they keep us very much in our comfort zones. And that means that we never have to challenge our own assumptions, let alone take the self-responsibility for attempting to improve our own life at work. We are powerless. We are weak. And you always know where you are with bosses you can't trust – you just don't trust them. . .

For some ways to break out of this self-fulfilling spiral, see Chapter 10.

We'll get used to it, if we decide it's what we want

Work and life, then is indeed a puzzle. But one whose ambiguities we'll get used to. Because the way work is for us now the result of how we have, over the centuries, agreed to think about work. And unless we decide to rethink the purpose of work and the nature of the people who do it, then the pressures and stresses of work will thus be carried into the future. But so will its opportunities.

Both Britain and the US have an aging population, but those older people are acting (and feeling) younger. More and more of us are going to be living alone, largely by choice. By 2010 in the UK, almost 40 percent of all households will be single person ones. For these people, work is going to be the central focus of their lives, around which other interests will be arranged. 2010 is not too far away. Already many of us regard self-development as a major outcome of our employment. People can see such rewards more clearly in the smaller companies (could see them most of all in the dotcoms) – but are the large organizations going to be agile and attractive enough? The loss of those with an entrepreneurial spirit from the large institutions could be the country's gain. In the US, one in twelve people set up their own business. In the UK, it's one in twenty. But rising.

There is a good news story too to tell about work. It is not all blood, sweat and tears.

As Richard Reeves points out, domestic workers are the most "satisfied" occupational group in the UK, whilst it's quite possible for a lawyer, for example, to find his or her work empty, dull and demeaning to their personal principles and values. Job satisfaction, and the link between work and self-esteem, is not an elusive chimera and Reeves – backing up Blanchflower and Oswald – has the data to back this assertion:

> "In a recent US survey, 83 percent of the population said that their work was an important part of their self-worth and in a poll by Robert Wuthnow, professor of sociology at Princeton University, 84 percent of full-time workers said that their work was absolutely essential or very important to their sense of personal worth. Of the respondents, 82 percent said the statement 'my work is very meaningful to me' described them well or fairly well."
>
> *Richard Reeves,* Happy Mondays, *Pearson*

Short-term contracts, and mobile, portfolio careers may be bad for the organizational social glue of trust, or they may not. Trust can be broken in nanosecond, but it can be granted just as quickly too – as long as both sides to the contract (whether a relationship or an employment one) are abundantly clear what the quid pro quo is.

More and more people will be happy to move from job to job, learning all the time, making themselves more and more employable and having fun into the bargain (because learning is fun). They'll have worked out that in the end the search for the right job, the search for the meaningful job, the search for the lucrative job, is actually what will bring the rewards. Work as journey and not necessarily destination: and a lifetime's quest at that (almost literally, since more of us will have to work for a living beyond what is considered the natural retirement age). But as Nordstrom and Ridderstralle remind us in *Funky Business*, mobility is a good sign, not a bad one: only poor and stupid people stay where they are.

Devising it all for Company

When I was about 16, my teachers made the rash decision that I should be made head boy. It was all a burgeoning teenage ego needed. One of the jobs I had was to choose the readings for morning assembly. I found, by coming up with sufficient *Bible* readings and extracts from Kipling and the war poets on a regular enough basis, that I was able to slip in, I presume undetected, recitations from authors of my own peculiar taste. I remember one time I chose a section from Samuel

Beckett's *Company* – a novella, as so many of his novellas are, about loneliness, fear, death and the remorseless if uncertain triumph of the human imagination. You can guess its suitability for a gathering of four hundred children aged eleven and upwards.

Anyway, I chose, on this particular occasion, an extract concerning the narrator's boyhood memory of a simple act of charity: *"You take pity on a hedgehog out in the cold and put it in an old hatbox with some worms inside..."*

To cut a short story shorter, the upshot of this episode is that the boy is fatally distracted by other boy-like entertainments and also by a "great uneasiness" that he should not have got himself involved in the hedgehog's destiny at all. *"That rather than do as you did you had perhaps better let good alone and the hedgehog pursue its way"*.

Some time passes before the guilty boy can finally return to the box. And things are a lot worse than he could have anticipated: *"... you have not forgotten what you found then. The mush. The stench."*

I know now that I must have looked up from this reading back then with an expression of solemnity and gravitas, a cosmic and teenage "so there!" to the assembled gathering. I also know now that I had no idea back then what on earth my text meant, other than that neglected hedgehogs rot if left in a box.

I think I now know what that story might be about. And in the publishing world's only known segue from the works of Samuel Beckett to Ben & Jerry ice cream, I'm going to let Ben Cohen speak on my behalf:

"As long as we operate within this old paradigm, we are separated from our heart and feel powerless. We cannot suspend our values during the workday and think we will have them back when we get home. We're all interconnected. There is a spiritual dimension to business just as to individuals!"

Choices for the Future, *Ben Cohen: Designing a Socially Just New World Environment (address to a conference of the Windstar Foundation, Colorado 1991)*

We can't expect a hedgehog to survive, let alone thrive, if we leave it trapped in a box. So too, we can't expect to leave our values, principles, our heart and soul, to be nourished if we separate from them for eight, nine, ten hours of every day in our work. Can our work be nourishing – for us, for others, for the world – if we do not bring our heart and soul to it?

It is difficult ground to be sure on, much less judgmental. I have seen in my own consulting practice individuals almost broken down by the strain of not being able to speak from their hearts, people forced (by whom?) to behave in ways contrary to their personal principles, with negative impact within and without their workplaces. And yet I have seen others thrive doing exactly that.

Just recently I met a woman who described in detail her healthy-eating regimes, how careful she was about what she put into her body. Her job, however, was marketing *Pepsi Cola* to the world, a drink partly responsible for the deterioration of children's dental health. (In the UK, a recent government survey found that more than half of children aged between 4 and 18 and two thirds of the 15–18 group have tooth decay and one third have unhealthy gums. The main cause cited was soft drinks and sugary food.) When I asked how she managed this apparent discontinuity between her own deeply held personal values and those of the company she worked for, she told me: "It's just a job. It's just something I happen to be good at."

Certainly individuals have different tolerances of what sacrifices and trade-offs they can make, and it would be unlikely that we could all find a company to work for whose purpose, strategy and values we were in complete concord with. But the ability to survive healthily in meaningless work, or in work which offends our own sense of worth and potential, is a rare skill which fewer of us have than we like to admit.

There has to be more to business than making profits. There has to be more to work than getting paid. To say that the purpose of work is to make money is a bit like suggesting that the purpose of a human being is to breathe in and out. Money is a natural outcome of work, but not the only one.

This does not mean that we are forced only to do work which clearly and explicitly brings good to the world, such as in charitable or philanthropic organizations. But it does require us to open up to the possibilities of work. If we demean work, make it a thing where the less of it the better, we demean ourselves.

If any of this chapter to date has spoken to you, you might want to contemplate the following:

"Work is a display of who we are. The work we choose to do, and the manner in which we choose to do it, reveals our self."

How is this true - or not - for you?

Rolf Osterberg writes "Work, as every other aspect of life, is a process, through which we acquire experiences..." What do your (good, bad, indifferent) experiences of work teach you about you?

"We cannot suspend our values during the workday and think we will have them back when we get home. We're all interconnected."
Ben Cohen

How do you align your own values with those of your organization? Do you have to compromise on some, at some time? Is that easy to do?

"The modern world takes a lot of care that the worker's body should not accidentally or otherwise be damaged. If it is damaged, the worker may claim compensation. But his soul and spirit? If his work damages him, by reducing him to a robot - that is just too bad?"
E.F. Schumacher

How does this damage show up in your workplace? What are the remedies and preventative actions you might take?

"I seriously question the spiritual and ethical life of anyone whose work has never gotten him or her into trouble - if no issues of conscience have ever emerged or no clash of values has been experienced with the ongoing guardians of the status quo. After all, it was Jesus's work which got him into trouble ... today every profession requires prophets ... no industry, no office job, no institution, no union will be exempt from a deep critique of its impact for generations to come on children and the environment."
Matthew Fox

How and when do you play it safe? How and when do you become a prophet for your profession?

A HIERARCHY OF WORK?

» Level One – working for the money alone, having a job, rather than a vocation or even career. Work as subsistence. *Feed yourself.*

» Level Two – working for satisfaction and growth. Accepting that work can be the source of self-esteem and self-worth. *Heal yourself.*

» Level Three – work organized, designed and delivered in such a way that it has the least possible negative impact and the most possible positive impacts on the family and social life of the individual. An absence of the stresses and pressures (inflicted by companies but also by individuals on themselves) which contribute to marriage breakdown, unhealthy parenting practices, addictions and other dysfunctional behavior. *Heal the family.*

» Level Four – work for the greater good; work which empowers individuals (particularly in developing countries or inner cities of developed ones) through education and development programmes. Technology which promotes and advances aid programs and sustainability. Acts of philanthropy and service. *Heal the world.*

Some summary questions:

Awareness is everything. . .

» What is work for, for you? What do you want it to give you?
» Who are you and how do you connect? In other words, what is your identity and purpose in the world – and how does that show up in your work?
» Have your worked out who you are working for? (To please your parents? To satisfy your bank manager? To fulfil an earlier ambition?)
» What are you good at, what do you enjoy, what do you find easy? Do you make a living from these activities? Could you?

» What would be the most appropriate expression of your talents – and in what form or environment? What would you have to change about yourself to make that available to you?

» What are you worth? How are you relevant – and therefore valuable – to the world? What do you need to do to update your relevance?

» Does your philosophy grow corn? Do you walk your talk?

» Ultimately, you can do no work alone. How can you improve your ability to influence others, and your capacity for understanding and exploiting the workings of groups and corporate cultures?

In Practice: Life and Work Success Stories

Three case studies from major companies who are attempting to create attractive, healthy organizations focused on the needs and concerns of the people who are at the heart of their businesses:

» SAS – strategic ping pong tables
» E&Y – big savings
» Capital One – a US experiment in the UK

The human relations movement of corporate history gave birth to various *quality of work* programs in organizations generally based on the premise that a happy employee is a productive employee. The new technologies of the nineties, as we have seen in Chapter 4, have brought enormous benefits, but also significant costs to the stresses and strains that people at work undergo (strains which cannot help but flow over into the private, non-work lives of those individuals). Add to this an even more recent business insight – that whether we are talking about customer relationship management, enterprise resource planning or business process engineering, the people are the most important thing – and we have the conditions in place which make the current obsession with work/life balance inevitable.

In 1999, the Work Life Institute of America published a report that highlighted the shortcomings of the work/life balance movement:

"Despite the wide range of work/life policies and programs available today, the existing policies still do not meet the need and, in many cases, do not achieve their potential value. Policies are rarely rooted in business strategies and may clash with corporate cultures ... Access to flexible work schedules, while offered by a growing number of companies, is often limited by the nature of the job and level in the organization.

"And while there has been growing corporate support for child care, the reality is that only a relatively small portion of the workforce today enjoys such benefits as on-site child care or even child care resource and referral services. While many US employers have implemented work/life programs and policies such as child care, elder care, family leave, or flexible work schedules, research has shown that such initiatives – by themselves – often have limited impact."

This report investigated how some companies have moved beyond simply adding a work/life program or policy. Instead, the

"employers in this study have adopted a strategic work/life-approach designed to accomplish a 'dual agenda': to simultaneously improve business results and employees' work/life integration. To achieve this goal, these companies have made systemic changes in their organizations – for example, through redesigning work processes, changing the organizational culture, or integrating work/life initiatives with core business strategies and human resource systems – rather than simply adding on programs.''

Like any fad or fashion, there are those who think they can take the shortcut, the fake-Armani route to looking good. *Work Life Balance* is just such a fashion. Yet there are some companies who have made significant progress – and achieved significant results – by moving beyond the ''here's the latest program'' approach and made the worklife issue a major part of their culture. This does not mean that you will find that all cynical voices stilled in these organizations, that all the employees are happy all the time there (that would be demeaning to the complexities and subtleties of that thing known as the pursuit of happiness).

This chapter looks at three organizations who might inspire individuals and other companies to reassess their own attitudes to work and life.

SAS INSTITUTE

''If you treat employees as if they make a difference to the company, they will make a difference to the company . . . At the heart of this unique business model is a simple idea: satisfied employees create satisfied customers.''

www.sas.com

It could be quote from a business consultant trying to inspire his audience to buy some common sense. But, for once, these are not the words of some guru, but a company who is truly living its message. SAS Institute has been in the top ten of *Fortune*'s ''100 Best Companies to Work For'' three years running and selected on the ''100 Best Companies for Working Mothers'' list eleven times in a row. But this is not a story of awards: it is a story of a pragmatic business decision leading to undeniable bottom line results.

From managers who work on projects alongside their staff members, to flexible scheduling that allows employees to work hard and play hard on the job, the environment at SAS is designed to enable employees to do great work and to have a life outside of work, as well.

SAS Institute is a $1 billion dollar software company in North Carolina, the largest independently owned software company in the world. Twenty years ago, six employees left to get married and have children. Jim Goodnight, SAS's founder and CEO, and David Russo, the company's human resources manager at the time, contemplated the prospect that the women would go on maternity leave and not return. It was not an option that the times made attractive – it was tough to hire great people back then too. So Jim Goodnight asked a question: "What can I do to help you come back?"

A quarter of a century later, 700 children come to work every day in one of three day care facilities in a company that employs 6000 people (David Russo set up the first one in a basement twenty years earlier for just five children).

Day care is only part of the Goodnight strategy to give SAS staff everything they need to do a good job. The list of benefits reads like a dream:

» a 35-hour full-time work week (the recorded receptionist voice mail at 5.00pm says "most people have gone home now")
» live piano music in the cafeteria
» unlimited soda, coffee, tea, and juice
» one week's paid vacation between Christmas and New Year's Day
» a 36,000 sq.ft on-site gym that includes two full length basketball courts, Ping-pong tables, a dance studio and a skylit yoga room
» workout clothes laundered overnight free of charge
» two on-site and one off-site day care facilities
» an on-site health clinic staffed with six nurses and two physicians
» free health insurance
» casual dress every day (except in client meetings)
» elder care advice and referrals
» on-site massages several times a week
» all family benefits extended to domestic partners, regardless of sexual orientation
» unlimited sick days, and use of sick days to care for sick family members
» Twenty-two and a half tons of M&Ms every year given to his staff, distributed every Wednesday.

In the cut and thrust world of software development, the industry average for staff turnover (SAS's competitors such as IBM, Ericsson, Nortel, and Cisco are not far away), is slightly over 20 percent. In 1999, SAS had a professional turnover of just under 4 percent, losing 131 people out of 3292.

And as a result, $75 million a year is not paid into recruitment, training and to the headhunters but instead goes directly onto the bottom line. What it generates in terms of two-way loyalty, personal productivity, and the benefits that accrue from keeping talent and knowledge in the company over time are less easily measurable but backed up by anecdotes from satisfied employees.

In many other companies attempting to implement worklife initiatives, claims are often made that such benefits as these are only available to a few staff members (the longest-serving or most senior people, for example). Not so here. SAS employs all its own landscapers, food service workers, housekeepers, and other support staff, and provides them the same benefits as professional staff.

Cynicism is not engendered at SAS, perhaps because there is no hint of cynicism in the way this company treats its people. David Russo, who was director of human resources at SAS for 18 years until last November, is quoted by *Workforce magazine* (March 2000, Vol. 79, No. 3) as saying:

> "This is not the good ship Lollipop. The benefits we offer are just the tangible stuff that represent Jim Goodnight's philosophy. A lot of companies think they have created a culture of caring, but the employees don't feel it. People put things together, but they are counter to the culture, and they are not being used. Jim's idea is, if you hire adults, and treat them like adults, they'll behave like adults."

CAP GEMINI ERNST & YOUNG

> "It's no secret that creativity, commitment, and morale all improve when people can work in an environment that recognizes active lifestyles."

Again, not a consultant writing a book, but a company facing up to reality and some responsibilities. These words are to be found on the home page of the Career Center area of the Ernst and Young's Website (www.ey.com). With refreshing honesty, they go on:

> "The reality is that, in our business, hours are sometimes late and workweeks are at times long, putting pressure on personal and family lives ... Our challenge is to keep solid contributors on board, provide the career platform they want, and foster the life they and their families need."

It is interesting to note, after hearing about SAS Institute, that another large professional organization should be provoked into considering a worklife initiative by its concerns over women leaving the firm. In E&Y's case, a female executive oversaw the change too.

Back in November 1996, Deborah Holmes the research director of Catalyst, a New York City-based not-for-profit organization that studies women in business. Catalyst had been hired by an E&Y task force led by Philip Laskawy, the chairman and CEO of Ernst & Young LLP, to look into the causes and solutions to some worrying statistics. Half of the $5 billion accounting-and-consulting firm's new hires were women, but the percentage of female partners and managers was not quite 20 percent. By the time you reached the very top of the organization, only 7 percent of the people at that level were women. Dissatisfaction with a corporate culture which was insensitive to the needs of individuals was not gender-specific, however. About 60 percent of the women and 57 percent of the men in senior management at E&Y told Catalyst that they were dissatisfied with working long hours. Each year, about 23 percent of the women and 18 percent of the men were leaving.

Catalyst recommended that Ernst & Young seek solutions to these problems on four fronts:

» Internal networking: Linking women across the firm's many practice areas and creating the support structure so critical to employee satisfaction and career development.
» External networking: Ensuring that women are used effectively in client development and giving women an appropriate role as representatives of the firm to the business community.

» Mentoring: Creating a culture in which the leaders of today understand their responsibility to help develop the firm's future women leaders.
» Life balance: Exploring ways for everyone in the firm to contribute his or her best to the firm while achieving a healthy balance between work life and personal life.

As a means of pursuing these recommendations, the task force suggested the creation of a group to focus on retention and employee-satisfaction issues. Laskawy asked Deborah K. Holmes to to head that group which was called the Ernst & Young *Office for Retention*. The *OFR* was established in late 1996 with a long-range goal to "have Ernst & Young the employer of choice among professional services firms for all people." In time, it grew to offer the following interventions:

Women's initiatives

Ernst & Young's *Center for the New Workforce* enhances women's career development and visibility, and leverages women's talents for the firm, through such initiatives as women's networks – action-oriented groups created with leadership support to enhance women's affiliation with Ernst & Young and provide opportunities for knowledge exchange. They take different forms – ranging from informal cocktail hours, dinners and retreat events to more structured monthly meetings governed by a steering committee.

[Since 1996, retention among women is up at all levels. In tax and audit advisory services, retention of women has improved sharply since 1996 – saving the firm an estimated $21 million.]

Flexible work arrangements

Currently, over 1500 Ernst & Young professionals, including many partners and both men and women, enjoy some type of FWA.

Holi-conferencing program

Through use of many E&Y video conferencing sites around the world, the firm has introduced its holi-conferencing program, so that executives working away from their families at times of national holidays such as Thanksgiving can keep in touch.

Privacy rooms

Ernst & Young's privacy room program helps nursing mothers, diabetics and other employees with special needs to integrate work and personal life.

EY/Assist

EY/Assist helps, as other firms' concierge services do, by taking care of those domestic matters (e.g., waiting for a workman to come and repair a leaking washing machine; finding the best school in the area for your 14 -year old etc) which would otherwise keep an E&Y employee away from the office.

Adoption assistance

The adoption assistance reimbursement program is designed to help defray the costs of adopting a child under the age of 18. Expenses can be paid up to $5000 per child, with an additional $1000 for special needs children.

Technology

Ernst & Young have a firm stance that technology is a mission-critical enabler and their philosophy is that it is not the technology itself that makes the difference – it's how people actually use it. Staff benefit from focused and "just-in-time" learning opportunities. Many of these are in traditional classroom settings, but often they are delivered through alternative training methods. These include computer-based training, video-based training, distance learning and self-paced tutorials.

But what benefits are there for E&Y?

By the end of 1999, 11 of the firm's 50 largest consulting teams and all of its 12 tax-and-audit practices had rolled out OFR retention initiatives.

In parts of the firm where there have been OFR prototypes, turnover has been cut significantly, work time has been reduced, client satisfaction has increased, and, as we've noted above, the number of women leaving the firm has dropped dramatically.

One particular success has been the 25 percent increase in people using flexible working arrangements. The education and expansion of this initiative beyond just "the lucky few" was aided by the use of two knowledge banks, open to all, the *FWA Roadmap*. The *Roadmap* is an interactive, electronic tool to guide people through the process of negotiating an FWA, while the database profiles 500 Ernst & Young people who use FWAs, and provides information in support of the business case for FWAs.

Knowing how others have achieved flexible work arrangements – and that they have done so without damage to their careers – makes it easier for employees who feel the need for an FWA to choose this option.

CAPITAL ONE

Capital One is a £2.7 billion (global) credit card company with 36.5 million worldwide customers. It has two sites, one of which is in Nottingham in the UK. It has many US-style benefits: share options for everyone, casual dress every day, above-average pay, pension-contribution matching, fitness centers, five-week holidays (four days can be taken on 30 minutes' notice) and community involvement in Nottingham, where it has its headquarters in Trent House, an old warehouse converted into an open, convivial space. Among other services, the company offers the family assistance program, a confidential telephone counseling service, managed by an external firm, that helps with issues such as stress at home or work, family concerns such as divorce or separation, and drug or alcohol abuse. All in all, it has been a very successful experiment in transferring a winning American formula to UK business cultures.

Capital One's respect for its staff has earned it a number of awards which the Capital One Website proudly details:

» 2001
  » *Computerworld* names Capital One on its list of the "100 Best Places to Work in IT." Capital One achieved a top 100 ranking for the third consecutive year.
  » Capital One is named top training organization by *Training* magazine. On average, companies selected to this list provided 66 hours of training per employee and spent more than $5.3 billion on training and development initiatives.

» Capital One received a national award from the Points of Light Foundation for its contributions to the community through its commitment to developing and managing effective employee volunteer programs.

» *The Sunday Times*, in conjunction with *Fortune*, ranked Capital One third among 50 best companies to work for in the UK.

» *Fortune* names Capital One one of the "Best Places to Work in the US" for the third consecutive year.

» 2000

  » *Computerworld* names Capital One twenty-third of its "100 Best Places to work in IT."

» 1999

  » *Washingtonian* magazine selects Capital One as one of the "Best Places to Work" in the Washington area

  » *ComputerWorld* ranks Capital One thirteenth in its list of the "100 Best Places to Work in IT."

» 1997

  » *ComputerWorld* selects Capital One as the "Best Place to Work" in financial services.

They also came third in the *Sunday Times* "100 Greatest Companies to Work For" list for 2001.

Since it began British operations in 1994, Capital One has captured 10 percent of all new card applications, making it third in the sector, behind Barclaycard and MBNA.

SUMMARY

The critical challenge for any organization contemplating an examination of its attitude and practices towards a worklife initiative would seem to be how to make it a part of the culture – an inevitable way of doing business at that company, rather than a plug-in add-on, the latest fad brought in by management.

The danger is that poorly thought through work-life initiatives, and, above all, those which do not genuinely spring from a profound acceptance that human beings really do matter, are likely to aggravate the very cynicism, exhaustion and feelings of exploitation that they are designed to counter.

As the Work Life Institute of America report says,
"The ultimate success and staying power of innovative work/life
strategies will depend on:

» building a broader understanding of how work/life strategies
  can address both business and personal needs;

[At Fleet Financial, a work/life redesign project increased flexibility
in scheduling and reduced the work load for underwriters by redis-
tributing administrative tasks and changing other work processes.
The intervention enabled underwriters to increase the time spent
on "real underwriting," as opposed to administrative tasks, and to
significantly reduce seasonal loan backlog ... The change initiative
dramatically increased employee satisfaction with the new work
system, enabled employees to spend more time with their families
and in leisure activities, and significantly reduced sleeplessness,
which had become a chronic problem affecting many employees
in the work unit]

» developing a chain of support and participation emanating from
  the top, middle, and grassroots levels of the organization;

[At Kraft Foods' Sussex, Wisconsin, pizza plant, workers who took
part in a high-performance work redesign developed a schedule
and a new team system that not only boosted production but
also reduced huge overhead costs and assembly down-time and
made it easier to recruit and retain people. It gave employees
greater flexibility and predictability in their work hours, making
it easier to arrange child care and transportation. It also provided
employees – many of them first-time job holders out of welfare-to-
work programs – with increased pay and training in business and
team decision making.]
and

» creating tools and practices to help other parts of the organization replicate the change process [as in the E&Y case]."

Finally, it might also be said, as the economic downturn spreads
from the US, that work life initiatives could well be under threat at

difficult times such as those apparently on their way. When staff are less scarce, companies may not need to invest as much in either attracting or retaining them. Such an economic decision – entirely understandable as it is – nevertheless only supports the generally held cynicism of most workers, that when push comes to shove, all companies really care about is profits. It will take some very courageous and humane organizations to buck this trend during a recession.

Key Concepts and Thinkers

Some key ideas defined appear in this chapter. It also allows the reader to look at the life and work issues through the eyes of commentators, authors and practitioners who are concerned with creating more human-friendly organizations.

AN A–Z GLOSSARY OF LIFE AND WORK

Business – From the Old English *bisig* meaning engaged, occupied.

Career – From *Romanic carraria (-via)* meaning carriage (-road).

Job – From the Old English *gob*, meaning a small parcel of something in the mouth. Later also a mining cavity and the heap of material mined from it.

Salary – From the Latin *salarius*, the word given to the payment made to Roman soldiers for the purchase of salt (*sal*).

Trade – From Old High German *trata* meaning tread and later track.

Work – From Teutonic origins, meaning engagement in activity

KEY THINKERS ON LIFE AND WORK AND LIFE AT WORK

Many of these biographies I have drawn from my own books *Smart Things to Know about Change* and *Smart Things to Know about People* (both published by Capstone/Wiley) but their relevance to the subject of life and work is clear, I hope.

Daryl Conner

Daryl R. Conner, "the undisputed guru of the change management movement" is the founder and CEO of ODR Inc., a research and development firm. Now considered one of the leading authorities on the subject of organizational change, he has taken his learning to the boardrooms of such giants as Mobil Oil, JC Penney, Pepsi-Cola, Levi-Strauss and AT&T and consulted to organizations and governments in Europe, Latin America, Asia and the former Soviet Union. The list of other major consultancies who have woven his work into their own is impressive – IBM, McKinsey, Ernst & Young – and one of the surest signs that he must be onto something good.

His stance is to demystify the uncertainties of the human change with clear processes and vivid concepts. Chief of these is what Conner terms "human resilience," which he says is what sets winners apart from those who are constantly feeling shattered by the increasing pace of discontinuous change. The five basic characteristics of resilient people are that they:

» Display a sense of security and self-assurance that is based on their view of life as complex but filled with opportunity (*positive*).
» Have a clear vision of what they want to achieve (*focused*).
» Demonstrate a special pliability when responding to uncertainty (*flexible*).
» Develop structured approaches to managing ambiguity (*organized*).
» Engage change rather than defend against it (*proactive*).

A strong picture of a resilient person is built up: someone who can expect paradoxes and uncertainty yet believes that even adversity is a teacher; someone who maintains the perspective given to them by a strong sense of purpose; someone who can display patience, humour and understanding when stress amongst others is high; someone who can shift their own frames of reference as the times demand; someone who looks for the common themes beneath myriad changes and applies thought and planning; someone who is happy to take risks and is good at getting the best out of the problem solving skills of the whole team.

That's an impressive list of credentials, and I'd suggest that more people can display them than many change writers would have you believe. But how many individuals compose their cvs to demonstrate these strengths? How many companies have a recruitment process designed to spot them? We still live in an age when we hire for skills and train for attitude. We employ, train and reward people for their ability to fit into a particular, specialist box and are then surprised when they have difficulty either accommodating or moving out of that box.

The shift seems to be to hire for attitude first and, where necessary, train to enhance skills. (Southwest Airlines, the most profitable airline in history, suggest this as being the lynch pin of their hugely successful, people-oriented culture. Read *Nuts! Southwest Airline's Crazy Recipe for Business and Personal Success* by Kevin & Jackie Freiberg, Broadway Books, 1997). Intuitively, you feel that's a good principle. I know many an IT director, for example, who would happily trade a half-dozen of his programming geniuses for a couple of Conner's resilient people.

Mary Parker Follet

Mary Parker Follet (1868-1933) is a much neglected management thinker and humanist:

"I do not think that we have psychological, ethical and economical problems. We have human problems, with psychological, ethical and economical aspects, and as many others as you'd like."

Born in Quincy, Massachusetts in 1868, and most notably a sociologist and a bluestocking social reformer, Mary Parker Follett graduated *summa cum laude* in economics, law, politics, and philosophy from Radcliffe College in 1898 and spent the next decade founding several Boston boys' and young men's clubs. This included the Roxbury League, which began the use of schools as community centres.

Like many other women of her class and intellectual achievement, she first went into social work, but unlike many of them, she took what she learned about human relationships and ventured far afield with it.

In her writings and lectures, Follett looked at such things as creative group process, crowd psychology, neighborhood and occupational associations, alternatives to representative governance, the self in the relation to the whole, and the important ideals of integration, synthesis, and unifying differences. Her focus was on the "community process" of "unifying differences." Follett spent many years writing and lecturing on industrial relations and management. Her advanced theory of management was based on motivation and co-ordination of group process. She emphasized the importance of relationships in organizations with her writings.

In other words, she was not only one of the first humanist management thinkers, she was also one of its first futurists:

"Reading Mary Parker Follett, it is tempting to think there really is nothing new under the sun. Warren Bennis writes that he finds her work, which preceded his own early writings by at least 40 years, 'dispiritingly identical' to contemporary leadership theory: she criticized hierarchical organizations and celebrated nonlinearity; she detested competition, bullies and the 'command and control' leadership style, favoring instead more 'integrated,' democratic forms of management. She thought front line employee knowledge should be incorporated into decision-making and suggested to companies that relations with unions might be improved if they tried to understand why a worker might want to make a higher wage or work in better conditions. Like most of her intellectual contemporaries she was in thrall to the new and hugely influential science of psychology, but she never forgot that humans are social creatures linked to other people by means of family and citizenship."

Barbara Presley Noble, reviewing Mary Parker Follett: Prophet of Management, *HBR Press*

Nevertheless, Mary Parker Follett has never attained the historical stature of some of her contemporaries. Was this because management science was, in her day, pretty much a men's club? (Her ideas became well known in Japan, the huge distance involved perhaps making her gender an irrelevance.) Certainly she was fated to preach her optimistic ideology of co-operation, negotiation, "constructive conflict" and consensus-making in a world that was either pre-war, at war or post-war during much of her professional life. As Peter Drucker points out, politically, the 1930s and 40s "were dominated by men and creed that knew the proper use of conflict was to conquer."

Michael Hammer

I remember hearing a tape of Hammer speaking back in about '93 (it was a bootleg of a business conference, no less – I have some sad friends) and being blown away by his humor, energy, style. In particular, I recall a description he made of a process driven organization where people were motivated to help each other, because such intimate connection is central to human nature "and human nature" he said, "lies at the center of the process organization."

And yet, and yet ... Michael Hammer was the co-author of the book *Reengineering the Corporation* and the patriarch of business process reengineering, a methodology so powerful that it persuaded hundreds organizations worldwide to lay off thousands upon thousands of workers. Mention Michael Hammer now in some parts of the US and they'll spit in your face. Reengineering, for them, means layoffs, downsizing, rightsizing, redundancies, early retirement, bitterness, anger, and despair. Who said gurus don't really change anything?

Reengineering traces its origin to the period in the 1980s when many large organizations suddenly awoke to the need for drastic improvement. In every measurable way, companies were letting their customers down. They were slow to respond, they were inflexible, they made stupid errors – and they charged their customers a lot for this service. People were focused on doing a good job in their particular area or function, and cared little for what was happening in the area or function next door, still less for a distant and anonymous customer. Reengineering shifts the organization out of this narrow, internal focus to looking at the larger picture which is the business process (input in, output out; raw materials in at one end, satisfied customer out at the other).

In a non-reengineered organization, people are made to look stupid or lazy or incompetent because of the number of mistakes, hand-offs, recycling of errors and the slowness and unpredictability with which the customer gets served. (Waste, he once said, is "marbled in" to organizations like fat in a steak.) Hammer's assertion is that all this is not in fact the people's fault, but the process's fault – and thus qualifies for his Pro-Human Award.

And yet, and yet ... the central paradox of Hammer's influence is that the efficiencies he promised through the potential of reengineering (potential being the operative word since up to 70 percent of reengineering efforts apparently fail) could only ever be truly delivered by cutting the number of people in organizations.

So is the world a better or a worse place for Michael Hammer?

Is Michael Hammer a story about reengineering at all? Or about the difficulty – and dangers – of applying theory in practice? Is it about business people and their relationship to business gurus? Is it about the human need to believe that something wonderful is always on offer? Or the fact that sometimes in life, shit happens?

Charles Handy

Charles Handy is a person who asks the big questions.

This calmly communicative and warm-hearted "social philosopher" (he long ago began to successfully blur the distinction between business concerns and those of wider human existence) began his expansive career at Shell and there learned much about the assumptions and beliefs which drive large organizations. Even in the past, he must have sensed that being big was not the way forward. He spent some time learning at MIT in the era of Ed Schein and other human relations experts, and took up a post at the London Business School where he taught from 1972. Handy has also been the warden of St George's House in Windsor Castle and a chairman of the Royal Society for the Encouragement of Arts, Manufactures and Commerce.

Handy's breakthrough book was *The Age of Unreason* in which he suggested for the first time and most strongly, that the only way we were going to meet the challenges of unpredictable, wrenching, discontinuous change was by learning to change ourselves. A new type of thinking and behavior was especially needed and a new challenge set for the smart careerist:

> "... discontinuous change requires discontinuous, upside-down thinking to deal with it, even if both thinkers and thoughts appear absurd at first sight."

Handy is not just content to label the paradoxes of our complex world; he provokes us to search for personal and organizational fulfilment and knows it can be achieved "if we can understand what is happening and are prepared to be different."

Handy's particular talent is for expressing possible solutions for the need to do things differently in images that have seared their way into the business literature's memory bank. Handy's is a world of shamrock organizations, inverted doughnuts, portfolio careers, Chinese contracts, sigmoid curves and empty raincoats. The latter haunting image, inspired by a sculpture by Judith Shea, expresses for Handy the fear that "if economic progress means that we become anonymous cogs in the machine, then progress is an empty promise."

Handy's writing is superbly readable, but "underneath its benign and positive style," as The *Director* magazine put it, "lies radical intent." His most thought-provoking work, in my opinion, is *The Hungry Spirit*, pushing us as it does towards a contemplation of "the meaning of business," without which all this change we're going through might appear an absurd and pointless nightmare.

> "What good can it possibly do to pile up riches which you cannot conceivably use, and what is the point of the efficiency needed to

create those riches if one third of the world's workers are now unemployed or under-employed, as the ILO calculates? And where will it end, this passion for growth? If we go on growing at our present rate we will be buying sixteen times as much of everything in 100 years time. Even if the world's environment can tolerate the burden, what are we going to do with all that stuff? Seventy corporations now rank bigger than many a nation state. Does that matter? ... The apparent lack of concern about these problems from those in powerful places smacks of complacency ... I am concerned by the absence of a more transcendent view of life and the purposes of life, and by the prevalence of the economic myth which colours all that we do. Money is the means of life and not the point of it. There must be something that we can do to restore the balance."

The son of a rector, Handy does not just preach. An advocate of challenging us all to know when enough is enough, he sits down with his wife at the beginning of the year and estimates what income they will need to do the things that they would like to do that year. When he has earned that figure, he flatly refuses to take on any more work, even though the temptation to give another lucrative speech to an audience of CEOs must be considerable.

Handy has a secondary career as a contributor to BBC Radio Four's *Thought for the Day* on the breakfast news program *Today*. His gently chiding has probably induced many a sleepy-eyed listener to think big thoughts – and ask big questions of themselves – as they make another dull trip to the office.

Frederick Herzberg

Frederick Herzberg's two-factor theory overturned traditional thinking about job satisfaction which assumed that one could either be satisfied, dissatisfied or somewhere along a spectrum linking the two. In fact, asserted Herzberg, a worker could move between satisfied and dissatisfied on certain motivation factors (such as achievement, recognition, responsibility and advancement) and from dissatisfied to no dissatisfaction on certain hygiene factors (such as working conditions, relations with the boss and colleagues, pay and company policies). The two-factor theory suggests that a manager must make sure that a job's hygiene factors are in no way deficient (so fair pay, safe conditions etc.) and then proceed to give employees experience of as many motivation factors as possible.

Rosabeth Moss Kanter

Rosabeth Moss Kanter is one of very few females who can challenge the likes of Peters, Pascale and Handy in terms of international influence and renown. Holder of the 1960 chair as professor of Business Administration at the Harvard Business School, she was also editor of the *Harvard Business Review* from 1989 to 1992. Under her stewardship, the *HBR* was a finalist in the National Magazine for General Excellence in 1991.

Like Handy, Kanter's writings are humane and grounded in sociology, opening up the potential for truly people-based organizations. Hers is the notion of the post-entrepreneurial firm which manages to combine the traditional strengths of a large organization with the flexible speed of a smaller organization. At the center of this is a positive reading of change. Look up "change" in the index of her first really popular work *The Change Masters* and you will find yourself directed to another entry: " *Change*; see *Innovation*," it says.

Kanter regrets the "quiet suffocation of the entrepreneurial spirit in segmentalist companies" and encourages empowerment: "the degree to which the opportunity to use power effectively is granted to or withheld from individuals is one operative difference between those companies which stagnate and those that innovate."

Lately, she has offered a four-part prescription for those companies which are intent on mastering change ("the most important thing a leader can help their organization do"). These companies, she says, must be:

» *focused*: to pick only those areas in which you can be excellent in all dimensions
» *fast*: to increase your innovation of goods to market speed, your processing of information and decisions speed and the recovery speed at which you respond and fix problems
» *flexible*: to employ the broadest of job categories, minimize bureaucracy and exploit cross-boundary team working

» *friendly*: not just the friendliness that aids collaboration within the organization, but the friendliness which build trusting links with their customers and suppliers.

She also adds a fifth *f* suggesting that unless corporations can maximize the pleasure and satisfaction that work can bring an individual, then they are not going to find anybody to do that work, because the pressures of change can be overwhelming. Her fifth *f* stand for *fun*, but I can't think that this is an idea that will ever catch on, do you?

Andy Law

Though only five years old, St. Luke's Communications has become one of the most talked about advertising agencies in the United Kingdom. It is an experiment in what a healthy and compelling organization could become. St Luke's is the only co-owned venture in the advertising industry. It wins numerous awards – though it doesn't enter contests – and it has increased its profits eight-fold. Chairman and cofounder Andy Law attributes the firm's success to its determination to continuously reinvent itself in a world populated by dotcoms and mega-ad agencies.

St Luke's intends to revolutionize the way business is done and provide a credible alternative to the capitalism of both the old economy and the new. Law sees business as

> "the most powerful force at work today ... [it] can treat you as well or as badly as it chooses. Yet we devote our lives unthinkingly to it, giving our knowledge, creativity and sweat without regard to its true value."

To bring back some measure of balance to life and work, St Luke's has chosen to turn its back on many business conventions and habits.

To this end, St Luke's pushes its people to take enormous risks, both in their creative work and in their personal development (a recent *HBR* article about him was called *Creating the most frightening company on earth*). As Law says: "We're fundamentally convinced that there is a connection between co-ownership, creativity, collaboration, and competitive advantage."

Kurt Lewin

Kurt Lewin, a German-born psychologist (1890–1947), has heavily influenced the whole field of organizational change. He founded a research center for group dynamics at MIT in 1944.

His most influential piece of research suggested that democratic groups work more effectively than those led by command and control, which is no massive insight now, but in an era dominated by corporate dictatorship and scientific management, his work was ground-breaking. The implication of this is that since a manager is not like a King forcing his will on others, he needs to be an amateur yet accomplished psychologist, understanding what people need and how they operate, in order to influence them effectively.

Two ideas in particular set Lewin apart as a major contributor. The first is the concept of force fields. Here fields of opposing forces hold groups processes in a state of equilibrium. "Driving forces" such as ambition, goals, needs and fears either move the group away from something they do not value, or towards something they do. "Restraining forces" conversely, oppose the driving forces – they might be characterized as apathy or group inertia. The two forces cancel each other out when they are equal and this is when a group achieves equilibrium.

In order to create change, then, we must strengthen the driving forces towards a better goal. Take an example with a specific objective. Introducing financial incentives to increase a team's conversion of sales is one alternative (threatening the sack is another). Removing "the restraining forces" in this example could be achieved by training the team in better closing techniques or in some other way decreasing the difficulty of the objective. Companies have been traditionally more comfortable with the easy option: if you want people to behave well, pay them a bit more. The trouble with this knee jerk reaction, Lewin suggests, is that it may have a short term benefit, but paying people more does nothing towards reducing the stress associated with carrying out difficult tasks. This stress may have damaging long term effects, and may also bind the team against the company. Individuals earn more, stress levels increase, morale plummets. It is a costly and unattractive option for the company even though it seems the easiest up front.

In this way, Lewin was one of the first to suggest that managing people was not about controlling them but about taking the time, and showing the care, to invest in their needs. More particularly is the idea that "resistance to change" might need not necessarily be a behavioral decision by a willfully obtuse worker, but may be present in the conditions of his or her job.

Lewin's second major contribution is the concept of a three part process in change: unfreezing the current state, moving it, then freezing it in a new place. While this was seized on as a logical and linear process of managing change, in fact Lewin again takes us into the complex and shifting world of group dynamics – and indeed into the same concepts that inform theories concerning corporate culture. He points to the shared norms, values and behaviors that any group establishes as being something that eventually becomes so habitual and comfortable that the group resists it against any significant change.

The routines and patterns of group behavior become a positive bond, and can only be lowered in one of two ways. The first way is by reducing the value of something which the group previously held as important. The second is by fundamentally changing what the groups values. Doing this, like most of what is commonly known as soft stuff, is hard work, but here Lewin returns to his democratic research. He finds that well-informed group discussions, at which the group itself decides to take on new values and behaviors is far more effective than a one-to-one coercive presentation by an outsider. Providing the information, creativity and safe space that a group needs to do this would be the sign of a good change agent in action.

Abraham Maslow

Abraham Maslow (1908-70) was on the faculty of Brooklyn College from 1937 to 1951. There he was mentored by the anthropologist Ruth Benedict and the Gestalt psychologist Max Wertheimer. Maslow so admired their professional achievements and personal attributes that he began to study what it was that made them so successful as human beings. His work in mental health and human potential was at odds with the study of psychology to date, which had focused largely on what was wrong with people who were mentally ill.

Maslow is most remembered for his concept of the hierarchy of needs through which he saw human beings' needs arranged like a pyramid or ladder. The most basic needs, at the bottom, were *physiological* needs - food, water, oxygen and sex. The concept suggests that as one set of needs is met, the person moves up the ladder to the next. In Maslow's concept, *safety needs* are next: security, stability, dependency, protection, freedom from fear, anxiety, and chaos; need for structure, order, law, and limits; strength in the protector. It is interesting to reflect on how far organizations play on and exploit this relatively low level human need. . .

Belongingness and love needs are next, and here we find the need for the recognition, acceptance and approval of others.

Esteem needs require us to have a stable, firmly based, usually high evaluation of ourselves, for self-respect or self-esteem, and for the esteem of others.

At the top of the ladder are what Maslow terms *self-actualizing* needs - the need to fulfil oneself, to become all that one is capable of becoming:

"Musicians must make music, artists must paint, poets must write if they are to be ultimately at peace with themselves. What humans can be, they must be. They must be true to their own nature. This need we may call self-actualization."

Self-actualizing people, he suggests, tend to focus on problems outside of themselves, have a clear sense of what is true and what is sham, are spontaneous and creative, and are not bound too strictly by social conventions. Maslow later redefined self-actualization as a function of frequency of peak experiences - profound moments of love, understanding, happiness, or rapture, when a person feels more whole, alive, self-sufficient and yet a part of the world and more aware of such high values as truth, justice, harmony and goodness.

Elton Mayo

Elton Mayo (1880-1949) created the Hawthorne studies, which called managers to realize that human beings in the workplace respond well to recognition, approval and attention and also to being part of a cohesive group.

So long as commerce specializes in business methods which take no account of human nature and social motives, so long may we expect strikes and sabotage to be the ordinary accompaniment of industry.

David C. McClelland

David C. McClelland is associated with human need theory, which asserts that people have urges (variously) towards three needs: the need for achievement (the desire to accomplish a goal more effectively than in the past); the need for affiliation (the desire for human companionship and acceptance); and the need for power (the desire to be influential in a group and to control one's environment). Studies indicate that successful managers have stronger power motives than less successful managers – so get the whip ready and practice curling your lip.

Douglas McGregor

McGregor's book *The Human Side of Enterprise* outlined a theory which suggested management behavior could stem from two opposing views of the inherent motivations of human beings. Theory X asserted that people don't like work, need to be coerced towards organizational goals and prefer to be directed since they don't like to take responsibility for their actions and destiny. Theory Y suggest that work is a natural part of life, that people will seek responsibility under the right conditions, and are bright and perhaps largely under-utilized.

Richard Pascale

"If it ain't broke, break it"

Richard Pascale made his name as one of the team of four consultants and academics who developed the *Seven S* framework – strategy, structure, skills, staff, shared values, systems and style – which any company is alleged to hold in equal consideration. Pascale's interest in the Japanese "economic miracle" of the post-war years led him to suggest that the Japanese success was based on their respect for and investment in the "soft Ss" – skills, staff, shared values and style – whereas the

West concentrated heavily on the "hard Ss" – strategy, structure and systems. Pascale later advocated the Japanese ideal of vision as a living, energizing action oriented *raison d'etre* – e.g., Kamatsu's "Encircle Caterpillar" – as opposed to the bland generalizations which typify Western efforts at vision.

Pascale's latest work has been into corporate transformation, which requires the involvement and commitment of everyone in the organization. Traditional change programs, says Pascale, are limited by the small number of people who are actually driving them.

Edgar Schein

Professor of Management Emeritus at the Sloan School of Management at MIT, Schein is widely regarded as creating he term "corporate culture." Certainly his book *Organizational Culture and Leadership* spawned a whole industry of books and research papers.

Schein developed Kurt Lewin's unfreeze-change-refreeze model. At the unfreezing stage, Schein points out that giving up one's attitudes and habitual behavior is painful, as any loss is. Schein believes that three process are involved to generate the readiness to change:

» *disconfirmation* by demonstrating the falsity of something held to be true and good
» *inducing anxiety* by underlining how personally damaging that loss of truth is to the person
» *providing psychological safety* to the extent that the person can accept that the new reality is inevitable.

In stage 2, change, people quickly try to bring back some stability to their lives, since the unfreezing stage brings significant insecurity. Schein suggests that two main mechanisms bring about this new stability:

» *identification with a role model,* whose own values and beliefs can be absorbed.
» *a process of trial and error*, where the person exposes themselves to a wide range of experience and information.

If any of this sounds to you like the briefing manual of a trainee brainwasher, then you get full points for your perceptiveness; Schein was involved in the debriefing and repatriation of prisoners of war who had been held by the Chinese communists during the Korean War. ''There's nothing bad about brainwashing,'' Schein is reported to have said much later, ''it's the Communism that was bad.''

Schein's work has a number of implications for people involved in change in organizations (and that means you):

» that a great deal of work needs to be done in informing people why the ''old way'' cannot and will not work any longer, perhaps as much if not more work than needs to be done in advocating the ''new way.''

» this is a difficult and sensitive task, because it induces pain in people, and is one that many would shy away from. It's easier to spend session after session extolling the virtues of the new world, because nobody's been there yet – there's little invested in it other than imagination. As such it's an impersonal, relatively safe task. Asking someone to give up the old world is tantamount to a personal attack – and too many people shy away from that.

» there are perhaps too many managers in old command and control cultures who actually would be quite comfortable with the disconfirmation stage; what many of us lack is the capacity for creating safe psychological space. Building trust and allowing difficult emotions to be expressed and explored may not be in your official job description, but it certainly has to be in your smart one

» walking your talk as a change leader puts you in place as an ideal role model for all those people walking about dazed in Schein's Change stage, looking for someone to believe in. The warning here, of course, is that they might hook up to another, entirely unsuitable role model. There's a great Dr Seuss children story in which a baby bird hatches from her shell, falls straight out of the nest, and spends the next 40 pages believing that, consecutively, a dog, a cat, a cow, a plane and a mechanical digger must be her mother. What is not funny is that people in need of a new role model often connect with the loudest, strongest voices, and amidst organizational change, those who are regarded as ''resistors'' and ''trouble-makers'' might well have those dangerous, siren and powerfully attractive voices. Beware of their influence, and act decisively to counter it.

» finally, Schein warns smart change agents that care has to be taken in the refreezing stage. Old behaviours and norms that still exist in the organization – or remind people of them – can pull people back to the pre-change state. (This is exactly what happens when you put yourself on a training course – you fill full of new skills and attitudes, and make a strong resolve to continue the improvement, but then find yourself gradually dragged down to everyone else's attitudinal level when you get back to work.) In your change work, eradicate as far as possible all reminders of old ways of doing things – old systems, processes, procedures, even artifacts such as time sheets designed in the old way. And if you are leading a change within a group that is part of a larger one that is not going through the same change, then pay particular attention to the boundaries between your group and the larger one. Brief your people to expect and resist the influence of the old ways. And use your powers of *coercive persuasion* (the name of another book by Schein, incidentally) to get the larger group on board as soon as possible

Peter Senge

Peter M. Senge is director of the Center for Organizational Learning at MIT's Sloan School of Management and a founding partner of the management consulting and training firm Innovation Associates. In 1990 he released *The Fifth Discipline: The Art and Practice of the Learning Organisation* (Doubleday/Currency) and instigated an enormous amount of discussion and theorizing about an entity which has almost steadfastly refused to appear. Learning organizations are a bit like the Loch Ness monsters. Everyone wants to believe in them, but very, very few have ever seen one.

Senge himself has an answer to this. "There is no such thing as a learning organization," he explains, which seems a pretty brave thing for a guru to say about the thing that is most associated with his name, and which earns most of his fees. By this he means that "a learning organization" is as much a vision as an external reality – and that what matters is the quality of questions and experimentation that the term provokes in us. Inspired by the search to become "a learning organization," many companies (Ford, AT&T, Federal Express among them) are making brave experiments in terms of communication, co-creating of vision, democratization, structural redesign and team working, and in particular being patient enough to seek the systemic origins of the problems they face, rather than hurrying to "fix" the problem symptoms as soon as they arise.

Companies are certainly moving a lot faster in these directions than they would have if Senge never coined the term.

Frederick W. Taylor

Frederick W. Taylor (1856–1917) was an inventor of scientific management, evangelist of measurement, efficiency and control, without much faith in human beings.

"Hardly a competent workman can be found who does not devote a considerable amount of his time to studying just how slowly he can work and still convince his employer that he is going at a good pace."

Victor Vroom

Victor Vroom (despite his comic name) developed the framework for *expectancy theory*, which asserts that people make choices from alternative possibilities of action based on how much they want a thing and how likely they think they are to get it.

Perhaps the single biggest truth out of these theorists is that high performance in a job leads to high satisfaction for it, and not the other way round. This underlines the need for smart managers to treat each employee as an individual and to act as a coach who brings out the best in them. People moving towards greatness (whatever that is for each individual) is what cultivates great places to work.

09.10.01

Resources

Who's saying what about life and work? Chapter 9 offers a variety of additional sources of information and inspiration for those taking responsibility for their lives and their work:

» books
» articles
» websites
» institutions

Material abounds, as you might expect, on the subject of Life and Work. Here is a brief guide through the data woods.

BOOKS

In this list I have only given title and author – all you'll need to find the books on www.amazon.com

» *Blood, Sweat & Tears* by Richard Donkin. Captivating history of work, by a UK reporter who leapt out of the rat race to write it

» *The White Collar Sweatshop* by Jill Andresky Fraser. Charts the changes in life at work over the last decade. Largely negative effects are concentrated on. "Essential reading for anyone concerned about the American economy . . . or worried about his or her own job."

» *The Great Disruption* by Francis Fukuyama. How "social capital" (trust, etc.) is breaking down in the current age.

» *The Reinvention of Work* by Matthew Fox. One of the few men sacked by the Pope – don't you wish you could have that on your cv? – writes a compelling, moving volume on the spirituality of work.

» *Funky Business* by Nordstrom and Ridderstalle.

» *Happy Mondays* by Richard Reeves. The director of futures at UK's Industrial Society suggests that work might be fun, in spite of it all.

» *Global Forces* by Bruce Nixon. UK consultant's excellent summary of the enormous changes people and organizations are going through – with some thoughts on what they might do about them

» *The Hungry Spirit* by Charles Handy. A provocative and passionate on the search for meaning in the modern world.

» *Dialogue: the art of thinking together* by William Isaacs.

» *Dialogue: rediscover the transforming power of conversation* by Linda Ellinor & Glenna Gerard. Two books about bringing people in communities of all sorts together in a fast-fragmenting world.

» *The He art of Coaching* by Thomas G Crane. A book about creating "egalitarian, mutually-supportive, high-trust partnerships between people that transcend the traditional boss/subordinate roles . . . this book is a clear guide for developing employees who are motivated, effective and happy in their jobs."

» *Bringing Your Soul to Work* by Cheryl Peppers & Alan Briskin. A practical guide to probing some of the personal issues we all have with work and how we decide to show up in the workplace.

» *The Art of Possibility: transforming professional and personal life* by Rosamund Stone Zander and Benjamin Zander. How to shift perspective on what's possible in our lives and work offering "an opportunity for personal and organizational transformation."

» *Maverick!* By Ricardo Semlar. An inspiring story of what can be achieved when a brave leader breaks all the rules, and begins to treat all his company's employees like adults.

» *A Simpler Way* by Margaret Wheatley & Myron Kellner-Rogers. A masterpiece, suggesting that there could be whole new ways of connecting as organizations if we understood and applied the natural principles of life – as gleaned from the new sciences.

» *Open Minds* by Andy Law. A story about the creation of the advertising world's only co-owned business, a compelling vision of what is possible when we let go of old assumptions about life at work. On the back cover of this book, Law offers the following advice, which I love and which I'm delighted to reproduce here:

TEN WAYS TO CREATE A REVOLUTION IN YOUR COMPANY

» Ask yourself what you really want out of life
» Ask yourself what really matters to you
» Give all your workclothes to Oxfam and wear what you feel is really you
» Talk to people (even those you don't like) about 1 and 2. (You should be feeling very uncomfortable now. You may even be sick. This is normal)
» Give up something you most need at work (desk, company car, etc.)
» Trust everyone you meet. Keep every agreement you make (You should be feeling a little better now)
» Undergo a group experience (anything goes – parachuting, holidaying)
» Rewrite your business plan to align all of the above with your customers
» Draw a line on the office floor and invite everyone to a brave new world

> Share everything you do and own fairly with everyone that crosses that line.

(You should be feeling liberated. Soon you will have, in this order, the following: grateful customers, inspired employees, friendly communities, money.)

MAGAZINES

Harvard Business Review

HBR have published regular, academically sound articles on life at work including:

» "Work and Life: The End of the Zero-Sum Game" by Stewart D. Friedman, Perry Christensen, and Jessica DeGroot
» "Must Success Cost So Much?" by Fernando Bartolomé and Paul A. Lee Evans
» "When Executives Burn Out" by Harry Levinson
» "The Work Alibi: When It's Harder to Go Home" by Fernando Bartolomé
» "Management Women and the New Facts of Life" by Felice N. Schwartz
» "What Do Men Want?" by Michael S. Kimmel
» "The Alternative Workplace: Changing Where and How People Work" by Mahlon Apgar IV
» "A Second Career: The Possible Dream" by Harry Levinson

These essays have been collected into a paperback book *Harvard Business Review on Work and Life Balance* which is available in all good book stores, as they say, and on the *HBR* website http://www.hbsp.harvard.edu

Fast Company

Fast Company has always majored on the personal side of work: the idea that work can and should be fun, energizing, liberating, a testament to our talents. They have not neglected to look at the dark side of "work is cool," which is that if you're spending all your time having fun at work, making all that money – and they're even washing your gym kit for you, then that's bound to have some impact on the you who has a life and responsibilities and interests outside of the workplace. Here are the titles of some of those latter articles: travel to www.fastcompany.com and key them into the search engine there to find the full texts:

» July 2000: "Stop the Insanity! (sane start-ups)"
» May 2000: "Jobs for Life" (Ernst & Young)
» May 2000: "You Can Do Anything – But Not Everything" (David Allen)
» December 1999: "Work and Life" (Helen Wilkinson, British thinker)
» July/August 1999: "How Much is Enough?" (*Fast Company* survey)
» July/August 1999: "Survey Says" (complete *Fast Company* survey results)
» July/August 1999: "Enough is Enough" (Canyon Ranch)
» July/August 1999: "The Way to Enough" (Norway's Norsk Hydro)
» January 1999: "Sanity Inc." (SAS Institute).

REPORTS

» Is Something Wrong with Work-Life Balance? A Look at International Data by David Blanchflower (Dartmouth College, US) and Andrew Oswald (Warwick University, UK). A June 2000 essay with some fascinating data that points out the disparity between some people's stated need to "spend more time with their families" and the wealth that they have in their bank accounts which should, rationally, allow to them to grant themselves their wish.
» Holding a Job, Having a Life: Strategies for Change A Work: In America Institute National Policy Study by Jill Casner-Lotto. This is a comprehensive report from 1999 on the work/life balance problem in the US and what at least ten case studies are doing about it. The full text is available for download at http://www.workinamerica.org/fr_holding_a_job.htm

THE WHINGER, SORRY, EMPLOYEE INFORMATION SITES

» www.disgruntled.com – though there's only a home page now with a link to book sales.

» www.jobhater.com – "The full-fledged site of hostility to the work-place." Say no more.
» www.vault.com – a huge, serious, seriously funded-by-advertising, HR/Career site, but with fabulous quotes from anonymous apparently masochistic employees on major companies' profile pages. Now you'll understand how bitter some people think their employers can make them.

INSTITUTES AND SELF-HELP GROUPS

» http://www.workfamily.com/ – an American site offering links to a wealth of information. The site claims to offer "the work-life field's most unique collection of history. Newly updated facts, opinions, research, company experiences and payoff for childcare, eldercare, telecommuting, job sharing, diversity, and ten other workplace topics, including a list of the nation's onsite childcare centers."
» http://www.worklifeforum.com/ – The National Work-Life Forum was set up in Spring 1998 by Joanna Foster. "It was born to stimulate change and it was founded on the belief that helping men and women feel more in control of their lives is good for society and good for business." Sponsored by some major European companies.
» http://www.employersforwork-lifebalance.org.uk/index2.htm – employers for Work-life Balance has been formed by an alliance of business leaders in the UK who believe that the introduction of work-life policies has benefited their organization. It is apparently supported by the Prime Minister.
» Finally, a more commercial site (0f many) to give the flavor of how private companies make a business of offering help to individuals and groups: http://lifeaccounts.hypermart.net/

OTHER SITES

Case study companies featured in this title:

» http://www.capitalone.co.uk
» http://www.ey.com/global/gcr.nsf/US/Life_Balance_-_Careers_-_Ernst_&_Young_LLP
» www.funkybusiness.com

» www.sas.com
» http://www.greatplacetowork.com/ – The Great Place to Work® Institute is dedicated to building a better society by helping companies transform their workplaces. Each year, the Institute works with *Fortune* magazine to select "The 100 Best Companies to Work For." The Institute also works with the *Sunday Times* (London, UK), *Exame* (Brazil), *CASH* (Switzerland), *Exame* (Portugal), and *Børsens Nyhedsmagasin* and *Oxford Research* (Denmark) to produce "Best Companies to Work For" lists. Links to these lists are available at this url.
» www.workforce.com – major HR/HR-related site with articles, features, reviews, tools etc. Recommended.

Ten Steps to Getting the Best out of Life and Work

Chapter 10 concentrates on the issue of work life balance for the individual – and offers both reflective and pragmatic advice. The ten steps are divided into some for all individuals and some aimed at those responsible for creating a healthy environment for others to work in.

It could be said that those same commentators, academics, management theorists and new leadership heroes (from Ricardo Semlar at Semco in Brazil to Andy Law at St Lukes in London) have overpromised and underdelivered. They attempted to deliver a global workforce, many of whom were battered by the downsizings of the early nineties, many of whom had hardly ever challenged their own Genesis-inspired assumptions of work as punishment, into a world of work which was rewarding in all sense of the word, where personal growth, creative endeavor and community were all available. Maybe they raised the bar too high – promising that which most organizations simply cannot provide.

What is certainly true is that the corporate cultures and management styles of the status quo are two of the chief barriers to all the possibilities of empowered individuals doing meaningful work. A company that still rewards and values presenteeism, for example, is hardly going to embrace the potential of homeworking, with its consequent benefits not just to productivity but self-esteem. At the same time, the corporate culture is us: it is the sticky amalgam of our collective beliefs, assumptions, rules and, most importantly, behaviors. We can't wait for the corporate culture to crumble without dismantling our own preconceptions and prejudices. Individuals must step into their undeniable reality, scary as it may seem: that they are, as they always have been, free to choose, free to create, free to act. In the next year, you'll have, roughly, 500,000 minutes alive on this Earth: how you choose to spend and balance them is up to you.

So here are ten steps to a more balanced reassessment of life and work. This advice is deliberately a mix of the practical and the philosophical – because you are that mix too.

This advice should be read in conjunction with the reflection-provokers at the end of Chapter 6.

MANAGING YOUR OWN WORK LIFE BALANCE

1. You can't create balance without considering the elements that we are trying to bring into balance

Many people bust a gut trying to satisfy the demands of work and life and wonder why they don't feel in balance – it's because they've left themselves out of the equation. This metaphor we hold of a see-saw attempting to balance work and home life is flawed – there's more than two areas of your life to be balanced. Where do you fit into your life? Too many business executives have left themselves out of the work/home/self triangle.

2. Balance is subjective and changes over time

There is no right or wrong balance to aim for, only what works for you at this moment in time. What is a good balance for me may not be an acceptable balance for you.

To achieve an optimum balance between your work, self and home, you have to work towards, and make continual adjustments towards, compromise. Sometimes, inevitably work has to take priority; other times your self or your home does.

3. Your intuition rather than your diary tells you when you're out of balance.

You could point to your organizer and prove to me that your life can't be out of balance because you spent eight days with your family last month. That's one story, certainly. Only your heart will tell you whether your presence in those weekends with the children was largely physical rather than emotional. Your body may have been present, but your thoughts back in the office.

4. Balance is about saying "no"

Sometimes you'll have to say "no" at work, at other times you have to say "no" at home. It's also about saying no to those things you originally said yes to – which is a bit like the process that goes on when you're trying to come to terms with addiction. You can't just go cold turkey and stop doing the things you said yes to – like that obsessive working schedule. You need to come to terms with what it was about that obsessive working schedule that attracted you so much and had such a hold on you. *That* is what you need to say "no" to.

5. Balance requires us to work in those areas in which we are most uncomfortable

Balance isn't just about time management: there could be elements of your being which are out of balance. Think of the numbers person whose left-brain logical powers become strongly developed at the expense of the emotional or intuitive side of their character. Coming into balance would mean developing right-brain aspects. Necessarily this is going to be an uncomfortable process because he or she is now working with areas which feel new or very different.

6. It is difficult to achieve balance without looking at the bigger context of your life

When attempting to balance the conflicting demands of children, work and your personal well-being, questions of purpose often arise. We move from "what should I do next" to "why am I doing this at all?" or "To what end am I working in this way?" Do not be surprised if people around you for whom worklife balance is an important thing suddenly start adding new activities rather than simply taking things away. They may well express an interest in performing charity, community or other works of service to others. Consideration of purpose often calls people to give something back to the world rather than looking to only take from it.

MANAGING THE WORK LIFE BALANCE OF OTHERS

If you are a manager of others, how can you create a healthy place to work by having the people who work there live healthy, balanced lives? Certainly there are initiatives and benefits your company can create – SAS Institute have shown that. But there is important work you can do every day to make work life balance a reality. You will need to demonstrate sensitivity and you will need to begin by building a bond of trust.

7. Talk about it

Give the subject of work life balance legitimacy. A whole raft of macho-management-dominated corporate cultures excluded the relevance of people's lives outside work. Work and life were separate boxes (in the same way that heads and hands in the individual were valued to the exclusion of their hearts and spirit). What people did (or could not do) in the privacy of their own homes was nothing to do with the company. Worse still, anyone in such a culture who showed signs of stress or breakdown would be considered weak and be made a candidate for expulsion in the next round of redundancy.

If you talk about work life balance, you make it acceptable as a goal. You also allow discussion of what gets in the way of achieving it, and what all of us could do to make it more likely.

Make it clear that your success criteria include two main elements: first, business performance and second, staff fulfillment. Underline that you will consider yourself a failure if only the former is achieved and ask your people's help in succeeding in both domains.

8. Personalize it

Since work life balance is a subjective thing and shifts over time, you must make every effort to understand the demands that each individual faces outside the workplace. Blanket initiatives must give way to flexible, personalized solutions. This does not mean gaining casual knowledge of your staff's hobbies or pets names, but a deeper understanding of the roles that people play outside the workplace and even the personal purpose and principles. What matters to them, and how can it be acknowledged (or even used) in the workplace.

9. Set compelling goals, but loose boundaries

Your job as a manager is to set high standards for achieving stretch goals which move the organisation towards its vision. But there is little in your remit which says you must tell your people *how* they are to achieve those goals. Getting out of the way of your people allows their creativity to develop (though clearly you need to be available as a coach when required). It also allows them to set their own constraints - or reinvent old ones. Take a very basic example: it is assumed that we all work the same hours (roughly 9–5 and usually Monday to Friday). If you never challenge the legitimacy of such principles, you'll only ever be reinventing the past as a manager.

AND FINALLY, REMEMBER GOLDEN RULE NUMBER TEN...

10. Life is difficult

Forgive yourself when life (or work) doesn't seem to follow the rules, when it doesn't seem to fit like it ought to - because sometimes it will, and sometimes it won't. Sometimes it's your fault and sometimes it's not. Shit happens. Move on.

Making a living should be important to you; but not as much as the work of making a life.

Keep experimenting. Keep smiling. But whatever happens, move on. You only have 495,995 minutes left after reading this chapter before another year is gone for ever.

This is not a rehearsal. . .

Frequently Asked Questions (FAQs)

Q1: Where did we get the idea that work was to be avoided?

A: Find out in Chapter 3.

Q2: Who has the most cutting edge ideas about what work means for the individual?

A: Find out in Chapter 6.

Q3: How can I get a better balance between my work, my family and my personal life?

A: Find out in Chapter 10.

Q4: Who wrote the most compelling research on the truth behind the work/life balance data?

A: Find out in Chapter 9.

Q5: What has changed in the world that we should need a book like this?

A: Find out in Chapter 2.

Q6: Who are the major gurus on this subject?

A: Find out in Chapter 8.

Q7: Life and work is an enormous, woolly subject. What particular focus does this volume take and what does that mean to companies and individuals?

A: Find out in Chapter 2.

Q8: How have recent advances in technology affected our work lives?

A: Find out in Chapter 4.

Q9: What differences are there in how different countries think about the life and work issue?

A: Find out in Chapter 5.

Q10: My company is thinking about launching a work/life initiative. What are current best practices and what are the main strategies for success?

A: Find out in Chapter 7.

Index